Child Training
FOR MOTHERS

Keeper'sBook™ series focuses on specific topics relevant to *Keepers at Home* readers. Our goal is to bring together talented writers who have passion for the subject and readers whose lives will be blessed by the information presented in each Keeper'sBook™.

© January 2021 Carlisle Press
All rights reserved. No portion of this book may be reproduced by any means, electronic and mechanical, including photocopying, recording, or by any information storage retrieval system, without written permission of the copyright owner, except for the inclusion of brief quotations for a review.

Editors: Marvin & Miriam Wengerd
Design: Larisa Yoder

Keeper'sBook™ is not sold by subscription. To subscribe to *Keepers at Home* magazine call 1-800-852-4482 or write to: *Keepers at Home, 2673 TR 421, Sugarcreek, OH 44681.*

ISBN: 978-1-933753-85-0

2673 Township Road 421
Sugarcreek, OH 44681
1-800-852-4482
Fax: 330-852-3285

Carlisle Press
WALNUT CREEK

Table of Contents

Perfectly Fit; From Heaven SARA BOWMAN ......Inside Front Cover
Parenting from a Place of Rest SHEILA J PETRE 2
Mustard Seeds *(poem)* LYDIA HESS 4
When Love Begins ANONYMOUS 5
Church Training ANONYMOUS 7
A Mom in Training MARLENE GRABER....................9
I Wish I Had Known *(poem)* ANONYMOUS................. 10
The Emotional Needs of Our Children HARVEY MAST........ 11
The Perfect Cake ANONYMOUS 13
Reliable *(poem)* LYDIA HESS........................ 14
To Train Up a Child ANONYMOUS 16
Dear Mommy ANONYMOUS 18
Confessions of an Overreacting Mama DARLENE ZIMMERMAN 19
Pieces BETHANY MARTIN 20
Too Darling to Discipline? EMELINE FOX.................. 21
Train Up a Child in the Way He Should Go! NAOMI MAST 22
Taught, to Teach *(poem)* LYDIA HESS 22
Light for Tonight ANONYMOUS 23
Prayer *(poem)* MRS JOE GARBER...................... 26
Basics of Godly Discipline MRS ESCH................... 27
Fruit in Season MW................................ 30
Out of the Mouth of Babes MARY E MARTIN.............. 32
A Life or Death Matter MRS G........................ 33
A Plea for Praise MRS HORST......................... 34
Like Mother, Like Daughter CHARITY MILLER............. 35
A Proper View of God M EBERSOLE 37
A Fine Line *(poem)* VIOLET MILLER.................... 38
From My Heart to Yours: NANCY STOLTZFUS.............. 39
No Time to Lose JOANNA YODER 41
Holding Her Heart from Toddler Through Teens RHODA YODER 42
Connected *(poem)* MRS JOE GARBER.................. 44
On the Same Side *(poem)* LYDIA HESS................. 46
Ten Tips for Training Tots and Teens ANONYMOUS.......... 47
Micromanaging Mom JUDITH KRAYBILL 50
Repetition *(poem)* LYDIA HESS...................... 50
Learning from My Father FAITH SOMMERS................ 51
Guileless Baby Boy *(poem)* RACHEL SCHWARTZ........... 52
Child Training Has No Coffee Breaks MABEL REIFF.......... 53
Wisdom Within and Without *(poem)* LYDIA HESS......... 56
The Biblical Recipe for Training Up a Man ANONYMOUS....... 57
Exposi-story *(poem)* LYDIA HESS..................... 59
Moods and Candy Canes JUDITH KRAYBILL............... 60
A Boy and His Anger J ANN.......................... 62
Teaching and Being Taught
    ANOTHER OF GOD'S CHILDREN IN TRAINING 63
Once Again LJ MARTIN.................... ...Inside Back Cover
A Mother's Confession MRS JOE GARBER .... Back Cover

CHILD TRAINING FOR MOTHERS   1

Parenting
from a Place of Rest
SHEILA J PETRE

Soon after our ninth child was born, a visitor told me how blessed she is to see "a large family of happy children with relaxed parents." Her words encouraged me, and at the same time challenged me; our children are not always happy and their parents are not always relaxed. The Spirit takes small spoken-in-passing words and drives them quietly home. He did that for me with her words, as I grapple with how to relate to the blessing of a large family. Can large families be happy?

What impact do relaxed parents have on that happiness? It is possible, even imperative, for a parent to be vigilant, diligent, and awake to the realities of life's struggles. But we cannot parent effectively from a place of desperation, reaction, or unrest. My children are happier when I train and discipline them from a place of rest.

Two weeks ago, we listened to a sermon about finding rest. These three things, the bishop said, are necessary to find rest: submission, commitment, and accountability. As I considered his words, I realized the same components are necessary for parenting from a place of rest.

Submission is not a mindless resignation to all circumstances. Submission requires active gratitude for grace within circumstances we cannot change, and a cultivated awareness of the ways in which we are called to alter the circumstances we can change. This means that if God has given me a large family, I will embrace the loud, crowded lifestyle that accompanies that gift without complaining how much work it is. Yet I will not just "submissively" assume that a large family has an excuse to be discourteous, neglected, or ill-trained; this is a circumstance I can and should change.

Some things cannot be changed. Who has sinned if a child has epilepsy or diabetes, the child or the parents? Neither—unless the parent resists the unfairness of the extra burden which a disability places on the life of the family. When I hold resentment in my heart against the ways in which my parents failed to teach me things which could make my life easier today, or that my child is naughty again, that resentment will be manifested in a sense of desperation as I train my children.

It's not my children's problem that they have so many siblings, or that I was not consistent enough in training them when they were younger, or that they were born with a bent toward sin. It's not your children's fault that your husband is ordained, that there is friction in the church, or that the income doesn't cover the expenses. We dare not take our frustration out on our children. A lack of submission to what God has allowed in my life results in a sense of desperation in all I do, even in my child training.

With submission comes unwavering commitment. When my husband and I chose to welcome children into our home, we chose to be parents for a lifetime. We chose to raise these children by following God's plan for the home. We committed ourselves to the work. This work includes love for each other, love for our children, and obedience to biblical standards of child training. We are committed to follow God's directives even when we do not see immediate results.

A mother who is not committed to parenting won't be consistent or vigilant. Neglect leads to frustration. When I am discouraged about parenting, my mother reminds me of the verse, *Correct thy son, and he shall give thee rest; yea, he shall give delight unto thy soul* (Proverbs 29:17). Life is a struggle; the Word tells us this. But it should not be an exhausting, draining, defeated struggle. If those words describe your struggle, something is wrong. Go for help.

Finally, neither submission nor commitment can be fully achieved without accountability. My husband and I choose to be accountable to each other—it's hard for me to hear my own tone of voice, and I can be blind to the ways in which my words affect my child. Michael, sitting by me at the table, can see things I can't—and I see things he doesn't. When we choose accountability, we open ourselves to advice and feedback, and remain open to reproof.

This vulnerability takes communication and humility. However, remember that some of us are too sensitive to criticism. We assume that every comment we hear that touches our parenting methods should carry equal weight. No. Oversensitivity can lead to discouragement, which is anything but restful. As you sift through which words to heed, give priority to those who are older than you, those who are parents, those who have been in your home of ten, and those who love you. The Spirit works through the words of others, but He works redemptively, mingling encouragement with reproof. When I hear the same admonishment from several sources within a short time, I know to listen—this is God's work in my life.

I have heard parents express desperation as they train one of their children. In those situations, deeper complications emerge years later. A child may be suffering from sexual abuse or dealing with emotional or mental handicaps of another sort. When you have a mentor to advise you, or someone outside the home to whom you hold yourself accountable, they may be able to see underlying problems which you miss. They may have advice for how to correct those problems.

One mother used an electric cow shocker in an attempt to prevent her daughter from wetting the bed at night. Another parent who heard of the account was distressed, but defended the mother, saying that "parents get desperate."

We cannot. *We cannot.* In parenting, desperate times *do not* call for desperate measures. Desperate times call for re-evaluation; they call for fasting and prayer. They push me to answer hard questions: Am I submitted to God's work in my life? Am I committed to His plan for parenthood? Am I accountable to another godly Christian for the way I am training this child?

PRACTICAL WAYS TO FIND REST

Stay in communication with the Father. Questions arise constantly; perhaps today your husband is at work, your mother lives half a continent away, and your wise neighbor lady is too busy with canning—you have no one near to advise you. You are not alone; you have a Comforter with you. Talk to Him. And then still your spirit to hear His answer. Be familiar with the Word, so that you recognize His voice and can differentiate between when He talks and when your own self speaks up.

Rest, literally. Sleep repairs the fraying tips of your body's cells, as well as the fraying edges of your day. *"This is not working. I don't know what to do. What is going wrong? Everything is falling apart!"* I rarely say words like these before lunch. I say them in the evening, and into the night. After fourteen and a half years of marriage, my husband has learned how to counter them: "You need to go to sleep." If I am chronically tired he suggests that I reevaluate my priorities and start to cut some things out.

Exercise regularly. Take walks—go out in the sunshine. Ask your children to go with you—or take one child at a time. Enjoy it.

Eat and drink well. Don't wear down your body with junk food and soda. Eat vegetables and protein. Drink milk if you can, and drink a little more water than you already do.

Follow a schedule. If you have a large family, you need them to help you with the work. My mother raised eleven children and taught us to work, though I did not learn to enjoy it till after I was married. She used colored ink on a grid, showing us which jobs we were expected to do in what spaces of the day. I construct work schedules on the computer, also with colored ink—one color for each child. When school starts, I modify last school year's schedule and tape it to the wall in place of the summer schedule.

Pace yourself. In other words, use a schedule for yourself. Since our baby was born in August, I have felt the crush of too-much-to-do-and-not-enough-time-in-which-to-do-it. A visit to my midwife confirmed my fear that I needed to slow down and allow my body to recover. So I've built a schedule into my day. Every morning, I tidy my house for an hour, and then I stop, whether I'm finished or not. Then I give myself permission to sit down and write a letter, or an article about parenting from a place of rest.

Establish margin. My best weeks are those in which I have a schedule for what meals to make all week. Then I plan my days more efficiently. If a child needs discipline twenty minutes before lunch, and I don't know what we're going to have for lunch, I may avoid disciplining, or administer the needed training too hastily.

Keep a tidy house. I am not able to keep a spotless house with an hour's worth of work each day, so I don't have new tips. I appreciate the housekeeping pointers which Dorcas Showalter outlines in her book, *Flourish*. Pick up a book on organization and browse through it, applying one or two points to your housekeeping. I value my mom's advice: *When you don't have time to tidy the whole house, clean one space of it well.* Make your bed. Keep your table cleared. Sweep the floor. Give yourself ten minutes to make one space beautiful. As you pass through your house later, you can rest your eyes, your spirit, or your body in that space for a moment or two, all day long.

Accept help. This is related to accountability. My baby was only eleven days old when our oldest daughter Rachael committed her life to Christ. In our community, such a decision involves making a custom head-covering and a cape dress. When my mother-in-law offered to help with the sewing and pattern-making, I was hesitant, even resentful. Did she think I couldn't do it myself? Well, of course I couldn't. I had a newborn and seven other children besides Rachael to care for plus I don't have my mother-in-law's skill with sewing. By accepting her help, I found space for more rest from which to parent Rachael's younger siblings.

Come unto me, all ye that labor and are heavy-laden, and I will give you rest. Take my yoke upon you, and learn of me, for I am meek and lowly in heart and ye shall find rest unto your souls. For my yoke is easy, and my burden is light (Matthew 11:28-30).

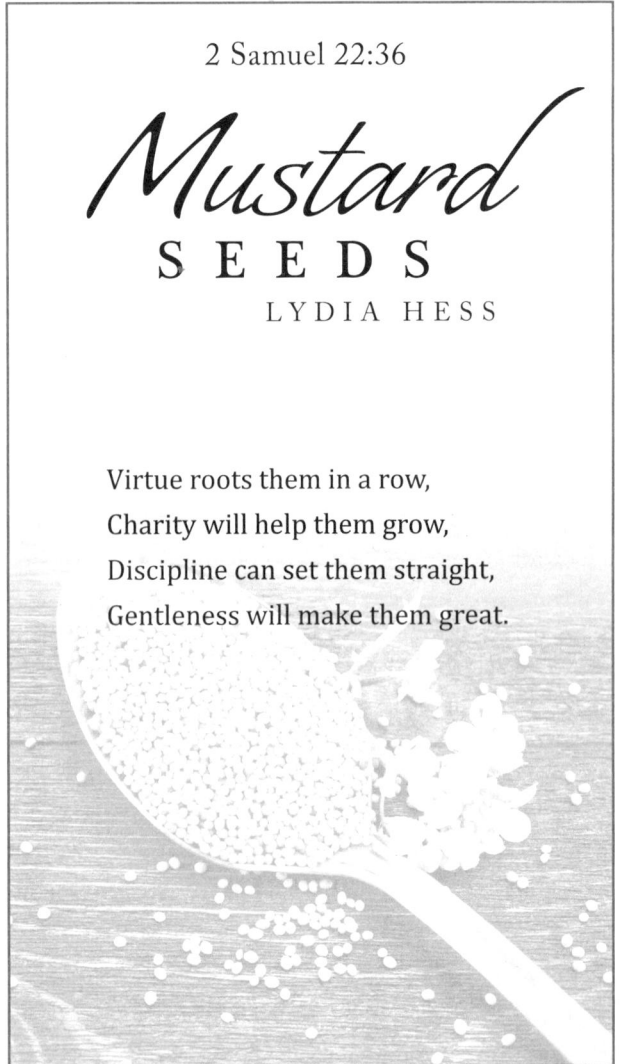

2 Samuel 22:36

Mustard SEEDS
LYDIA HESS

Virtue roots them in a row,
Charity will help them grow,
Discipline can set them straight,
Gentleness will make them great.

When Love Begins
ANONYMOUS

Dear Mama,
I hear the sweet nothings you whisper into my ear and I feel your kisses on my cheeks. When you pat my back, rocking me to sleep, I feel your love. I stop fussing when you reach for me, taking me from my sibling's arms; it's then that you make me feel loved and safe. I taste your sweet milk. I gaze into your face, when I see those smiles that are meant just for me. I know you love me now.

Mother, when did your love for me begin?

Those early weeks, when you hoped and hoped that you were just "late" or that you had miscalculated or that you had just "skipped," when you pushed off taking a test because you did not want to know about me, did you love me then?

When you were finally certain about me, when you saw the two pink lines that confirmed a brand-new life and you cried to Daddy, or became discouraged, or upset, did you love me then?

When did you start loving me, Mama? When do you think God wanted you to start loving me?

I am your gift from God,
Your own sweet Babe

How we feel toward our unborn children may have more of a lasting effect than we might imagine. Adults who have more than the usual amount of struggles—those who often end up staying at those places that help people with mental and emotional difficulties—can often trace their negative or destructive feelings or thought patterns back to early feelings of rejection from their own mothers. This is true in our plain circles as well as in the secular world.

After taking many courses in the care of foster and adoptive children, we have heard the results of various secular studies on the subject of the maternal-infant connection. A wide variety of studies who tracked children from conception into middle age all showed similar, interesting results.

The simplest way to show these results is to draw a circle and then divide it into thirds. They conclude that the first one-third of how an adult turns out is from his genetics. For instance, if a child's biological parents or grandparents are prone to be talkative, shy, fast, slow, creative, graceful, loud, quiet, heavy, or many other traits, the child may inherit these traits through genetics alone, even if they are not raised by their biological parents.

Furthermore, their studies show that a full one-third of how a child develops as an adult has to do with his experiences in his mother's womb. They believe that unborn children can feel love, acceptance, rejection, indifference, fear, anxiety, trauma, and many other feelings from its mother.

One interesting example of this (many lifetime studies were done on these babies) was when President John F. Kennedy was assassinated. A very large amount of these unborn children—regardless which stage of the pregnancy the mothers were in—had more problems with anxiety and depression, when compared with those who were conceived after or those born before that tragic event.

Not only mental and emotional problems were linked to before-birth experiences, but also other things like learning problems, attachment issues, eating disorders, and more.

In the conclusion of these studies, only the last one-third of an adult's makeup and traits can be contributed to the care, nurture, teaching, love, admonition, training, and acceptance he or she receives after birth. (These studies do not include those infants who are affected by drugs or alcohol use before birth, in which case, before-birth experience contributes to more than one-third.)

Another interesting factor for those conducting these findings has been the study of those children who are placed in loving, adoptive homes, at or soon after birth. Many of these babies received excellent care by mothers who dearly wanted babies. Those that had more than the usual amount of difficulties were the ones with birth mothers who were indifferent, disturbed, or upset toward their unborn children.

On the other hand, when the biological mothers wanted and loved their unborn babies, but gave them up for adoption for financial, social, or other reasons—those babies had significantly less problems than those whose mothers did not love their babies while they were in utero.

While these types of studies are interesting and probably hold a considerable amount of truth, can we put full trust in these studies alone?

Let us turn to the truth of God's Word. Psalm 139:13-17 reads, *For thou hast possessed my reins: thou hast covered me in my mother's womb. I will praise thee; for I am fearfully and wonderfully made: marvellous are thy works; and that my soul knoweth right well. My substance was not hid from thee, when I was made in secret, and curiously wrought in the lowest parts of the earth. Thine eyes did see my substance, yet being unperfect; and in thy book all my members were written, which in continuance were fashioned, when as yet there was none of them.*

We can understand that God has His hand over us even while we are in our mother's womb. Have you ever seen the pictures of a life that has just begun? A cell divides into two then those into four. Cells become skin and organs and intricate features; limbs and hair are formed. Aren't these miracles fearful and wonderful and marvelous? These miracles that happen in secret are not hid from God's eyes. In His book all our features are written, even while they continue to be fashioned; yes, even before they are even there. Isn't it remarkable that God creates life in such a miraculous way, and while it is being created, He keeps his hands over it?

If He keeps his hands over a new life, He must love it and so should we.

What if we have failed? What if we miserably rebelled against a new pregnancy? This is where secular circle graphs miss out on the greatness of our heavenly Father. We have a Father who is exceedingly merciful. He extends grace for all our failures if we are repentant. Even if we struggled with the fact that we were given a new life to hold and take care of for our entire pregnancy, we can ask God's forgiveness. As soon as forgiveness begins, redemption begins. Even while we rejected a pregnancy, we can love our child. We can tell them many times that we are thankful that we have them as part of our family and that they are a gift from God.

In my own story, I often heard my mother say that she thought she had family planning figured out and she never wanted another baby. Many years later, I sat with a counselor one day, trying to figure out why I was struggling with life so much. Somewhere from deep within me words were formed and came spilling out in a torrent of tears. "My mother always said she never wanted another baby. I don't think she—she ever—ever loved me," I wailed. That day forgiveness and healing in my heart began. I believe if my mother could have added to that oft-repeated refrain, "But I am thankful that we have you," it would have done much to take away those feelings of rejection.

It may not be too late for you. Tell your children that you love them. Tell them that God planned for them and secretly decided just how they would look before they were born. Tell them that God loved them when they were still very, very tiny. Yes, often, tell them that you love them. In so doing you may be able to repair, redeem, replace, re-love any unloving feelings you had at the start.

Leave their genetics to God. Work on their after-birth nurturing and training every day. And for the other one-third, before they are born, ask God to help you love them, even as He does.

CHURCH TRAINING

ANONYMOUS

"Wait a minute, sir." The interment for our elderly neighbor had ended, and we were walking back to our vehicle. The Baptist pastor hurried to our side. "I want to shake your hand." He pumped Dave's hand heartily and leaned in close. "I've been watching your family all morning, sir. I have never in my life seen such well-behaved children. Even this little one didn't make a squeak. Please, what is your secret?"

Dave smiled. "Oh, it's not us doing anything spectacular. We're only trying to follow the Bible way."

"Sure, sure," the pastor agreed. "You're obviously doing something right. God bless you!"

I waited until we were in the van and out of earshot to breathe, "Wow."

"To God be the glory," Dave added humbly.

Our twenty-month-old did sit quietly through the hour-long funeral service. One hour was easy—he was used to enduring Sunday morning services twice that long. Our other four children sat on either side of us silently watching the unusual proceedings. I hadn't given it a thought. But now I did. Was there, like the Baptist pastor implied, a secret to it? Yes, we strive to follow the Bible way. Yet what exactly is the formula for teaching a child to behave in church?

Several weeks later, still mulling over the principles, an opportunity arose to try putting them into words. "Tell me," the sincere young mother pleaded. "How do you get your little boy to sit so still in church?"

Lyle and Sharon were part of a different church constituency and had attended our Sunday morning service. Now it was after lunch, and Sharon and I were enjoying the breeze on our shady front porch. *What should I say, Lord?* I hurriedly pulled my thoughts together. Sitting beside Sharon in church that morning, I had tried not to inwardly criticize as her fourteen-month-old and my four-year-old received nonstop entertainment.

Little Suzanne was a handful in church, Sharon had lamented afterwards. She certainly was. But I could hardly blame Suzanne. Why not fuss? Every time she did, out came a new toy to play with. *Please, Lord, keep me from sounding like a know-it-all.*

"I don't have the last word on the subject," I said wanting to make that clear. "Anything we've learned is from the Lord."

"Of course. But your little Lyndon is obviously under control. Do you have sitting-still sessions with him at home each day?" Sharon wondered. "I've read about those. Maybe I should try it."

"No, I never have." I smiled at her surprise. "But," I hastened to add, "when ours are around six months old, Dave takes them during family devotions and holds their hands together. At our stage of family life, that lasts about fifteen minutes."

"So training them to sit still early is more effective than waiting till they're a year old?"

"It has worked that way for us." I chewed my lip as I contemplated how to go on. There were other aspects to cover about church training.

"Come on, say it," she said with a grin.

"Who said I had anything more to say?"

"It's plain as day. Go on. I'd rather be told straight out than have somebody beat around the bush."

"I love your attitude," I commended. "I'm too easily offended. But if you want to know exactly what I'm thinking, here goes. Church toys aren't necessary."

To my amazement, Sharon agreed. "I thought you'd say that. At our church, everybody takes bulging diaper bags—let's just call them entertainment bags—for their little folks. So I have, too. But I'm beginning to wonder whether it's a good idea. Are you really sure Suzanne would be more content without toys?"

I nodded. "I'm really sure. Toys work against what you are trying to teach her—to sit still. And each toy only lasts a little while until your child wants another one."

"Do I ever know that!" Sharon sighed. "So you never take toys to church?"

"I'll take beads for a small baby, maybe a four-month-old, but that's all. And someone paved the way before us," I added. "None of the parents in our church bring those bulging diaper bags you mentioned. So we had it easy. We saw it working for others, and now it works for us."

"What else?" Sharon wondered. "I noticed Lyndon sat with his daddy through the whole service. Is that your next point?"

"You're a good guesser!" I watched the children playing together at the other end of the porch as I formulated my next bit of advice. "Babies who are getting bored or tired in church automatically think, *I want to nurse*, when they're sitting with Mom. And we softhearted moms usually give in. But a one-year-old who's filled his tummy before church can easily go all morning without a fill-up when he's with Daddy."

"When do yours start sitting with Dave for the whole service?"

"It depends on the child. Usually around a year old. The first few times he always needs to take them out for discipline. But after several Sundays, those trips outside become rare. Baby learns that there isn't any option except sitting quietly, and most times he ends up falling asleep on Dave's lap."

Sharon sighed again. "It sounds marvelous. I'd like to try this approach with our next baby, but I'm afraid it's too late for Suzanne. She just cries when Lyle takes her in church."

"Oh, it's not too late," I assured Sharon quickly. "She's only fourteen months old. There may be a struggle, but she can still learn to be happy with her daddy. You'll have to sit somewhere that she can't easily see you until she adjusts to it. But you'll find it so relaxing to let your husband's strong arms handle her."

Sharon was silent a few minutes, sorting her thoughts. "So," she summed up our discussion. "Start young, no toys, and sit with Daddy. It *sounds* simple, at least. Anything else?"

I couldn't help chuckling. "Your candor is refreshing. And I can see you're getting it. But wait—how about some popcorn and lemonade before we go on?"

"Oh, dear! Is it going to get that much deeper?"

"No. We're almost done. But I'm thirsty from all this talking."

Ten minutes later we were back on the porch, situating the children around the picnic table with their own bowls of popcorn. "One more point for older children," I continued when we were back on the porch swing. "Some children carry a little New Testament to church long before they can read it. When I suggested getting one for our oldest, Dave asked, 'Why? What is it for?' I had to admit it is only a plaything. Instead, we give our children a real church Bible on their seventh birthdays."

"I never thought about the disconnect in giving Bibles to children before they can read," Sharon said thoughtfully. "But I have been bothered by the way those Bibles are treated. Small children don't know how to handle the Bible with proper respect."

"Great thought," I praised. "That aspect hadn't even entered my mind. See, you're teaching me now."

Sharon beamed. "My pleasure! It's about my turn, isn't it?" she teased.

We laughed together. Then I sobered as the weight of her insight struck me. "And really, Sharon, doesn't that encapsulate the whole reason for teaching our children reverence in church? So they learn, like you said, the proper respect for God's Word, His house, and for God Himself?"

Pensively, we reflected on the importance of teaching children respect for God. The door opened then, and the men stepped out on the porch.

"I could see through the window that you ladies were in pretty deep." Lyle grinned. "Are you anywhere close to wrapping it up?"

Sharon smiled and turned to me. "Are we?"

"Oh, I'd say so. But I hope you can come again sometime. I've thoroughly enjoyed the afternoon."

"Same here. And I've learned a lot." Sharon helped me carry the glasses and popcorn bowls to the kitchen. "Thanks so much for all you've shared."

My heart was full as we watched them drive away. Dave took Sharon's place on the porch swing and we shared notes on our afternoon discussions. Interestingly, Dave and Lyle had also covered the church-training topic. "It was good for me to review these principles," I finished, "and to be reminded of the actual goal—teaching our children respect for God."

Dave ate the last of the popcorn. "Same here. Let's pray for Lyle and Sharon and other young parents as they strive for more peaceful church services."

"Certainly. And Dave," I said, laying my hand on his knee. "I'm so thankful to be part of a church and married to a man who make practicing these simple rules just that—simple."

Dave smiled and said, "To God be the glory."

A Mom in Training

MARLENE GRABER

Our lighthearted conversation held no steady rhythm. My husband was stretched on the couch, browsing through a hunting magazine, while I walked around the house picking up baby blankets, coats, scattered shoes, and anything else that got carried in from the garage.

"I stopped at Karen's house today," I commented to my husband. "And there was no sense in how things looked at her house!" Picking up my family's belongings had made me think about it.

"Her children were riding bikes right over the tops of blankets and coats! There were shoes everywhere, the kitchen was a total clutter of everything, and there was even an open bag of chips, mashed in a trail beside the living room couch. Really, it was unnecessary. She has three school-age children who are totally capable of helping somehow, surely."

I went on to mention that I do understand it is impossible to have all things perfect, and that *one* mom in a home with *eight* children is an uneven yoke. I very well understand the need to let some things go as you focus on another, or that sometimes you simply need sleep more than order. I *get* all this. I am a mom.

"But I pondered this all afternoon," I rambled on to my husband, unsure if he was even listening to me. "Does it really have to be this way? Is it really completely hopeless at that stage in life? Is it not possible to raise a family yet still *keep a home*?" I cast a quick glance at the dishes stacked in *my* sink, the toys scattered on *my* floor.

I have three children at this point and it was clear that if I didn't change something, I would be in my friend's shoes if I ever had eight children.

Then God gave me a vision. A goal. God gave me wisdom in a Proverbs verse stating: *Train up a child…*

A house is a home when the family's all gathered comfortably together, but a *clean* house is part of that comfort! At a very young age, children can be taught to pick up their own belongings. It's a simple act of training them responsibility. When my son comes home from school, drops his coat right inside the door, plops his lunch pail and books on the cupboard, and slips off his shoes under the table while eating a snack, it is lack of proper training. When my daughter dumps her doll tote on top of the box of blocks and leaves the mess to go look at books, it is lack of proper training. When we finish a meal and everyone walks to the living room after dismissal prayer, leaving Mom to stare at all the dishes, it is lack of proper training.

Consistency is the key! Again and again, over and over. *Train up a child!* It is easy for me to meet my school boy at the door and promptly pick up his coat as he drops it. It's easy to follow his trail, picking up everything he lays down. It actually saves time! It definitely takes more effort to train, but it's beneficial for both of us in the long run. After a solid week of meeting him at the door and enforcing that he take the extra ten steps over to the coat hooks and hang his coat *properly* (not tossing it from three feet away, hoping it lands somewhere amidst the hooks!), it becomes a new habit. Now, when he walks in the door, he naturally—instinctively—walks directly to the hooks without thinking. I watch and I marvel. All it took was a little effort, a little proper training. Rome wasn't built in a day. Neither is life

continued on page 12

I Wish I Had Known

ANONYMOUS

I read it again, and stopped in my tracks.
Had I missed—all these years—such an obvious fact?
Remorse filled my heart, and scene after scene
Flashed through my mind till I felt awfully mean…

The times he'd been dirty and wet to the core,
And mud prints his size marched past on the floor,
While he glowingly told of his new fishing line—
Or the boat he had built which he thought was quite fine.

He once planted trees with acorns and spade.
He once called me out to the flower bed he'd made.
He'd given me flowers, and stones, and nice sticks,
And salvaged my junk that he wanted to fix.

Time after time of just being a boy
Time after time of looking for joy—
His God-given instinct had brought him to me,
And most of those times… How could I not see?

I had moaned at his dirt and the laundry it caused.
I had scolded his tracks and then barely paused
To listen to stories he wanted to say,
While wishing inside that he'd go on his way…

But now I am stricken. I see I have failed.
I've squandered the moments that might have been filled,
With knitting of heartstrings—my son's to my own—
The best years are gone now. I wish I had known…

It said, "*In the heart of each little boy*
Is a desire to please; to bring special joy
To a female. God purposely made him that way,
'Twill work as the glue in his marriage someday."

And he comes to the one who should love him the best.
Applaud his good points; accept all the rest.
If his mama won't do this, where should his heart go?
Forgive me, dear God! I wish I had known.

The Emotional Needs of Our Children

HARVEY MAST

Luke 11:11: *If a son shall ask bread of any of you that is a father, will he give him a stone?*

Our children have physical needs, so we give them food to eat and clothes to wear. They have spiritual needs, so we lead them to God. But they also have emotional needs. How are we meeting those needs?

Mark 10:13: *And they brought young children to [Jesus], that he should touch them... 16 And he took them up in his arms, put his hands upon them, and blessed them.*

What do you think that did for the emotional health of those children?

How can *we* bless our children in a way that they feel secure under our protection and guidance? What are some practical ways in which we can meet the emotional needs of our children?

1. Physical Contact

The folks that brought those children to Jesus understood that physical contact is important to a child: *they brought young children to him, that he should* touch *them.* And Jesus *took them up in his arms, and put his hands on them.*

The foundation for a child's security is established by the physical contact we give them when they are young. A young child needs his parents to touch, hold, and cuddle him. A normal child feels secure when we express our love to him through physical touch.

2. Respectful Conversation

We meet the emotional needs of our children when we talk with them. Talk to your child. Give him your full attention when he is talking to you. Try to see things through his eyes. Hear, observe, and perceive his spirit. Connect with your child's heart.

When we establish open and mutually respectful dialogue with our children, we show them that we value and accept them. Take time to talk to your children.

3. A Stable Environment

A stable environment contributes to a child's emotional health. Parents who are calm and steady amidst life's chaos contribute to their child's emotional stability. But a parent's extreme reactions or unjust punishments can undermine the child's emotional stability.

Clear rules can be stabilizing. A child is more settled and secure when he knows what behavior is acceptable and what behavior is not acceptable. But rules can only create a stable environment when parents enforce them. And that brings us to punishment.

4. Loving Punishment

According to the world, punishment shows a lack of love. But the rod in a parent who is full of God's Spirit and the love of Christ brings security to a child and frees him from guilt.

Children wallow deeper and deeper into the misery of selfishness if parents do not free them from guilt. Left unchecked, a selfish child will destroy himself while annoying those around him.

Loving parents want a relaxed, respectful relationship with their children. Disobedience strains this relationship. A parent who truly loves his child takes the initiative to restore their relationship by administering loving punishment. Given in this context, punishment contributes to the child's emotional well-being.

5. Fear Management

Fear management is not always fear elimination. Appropriate fears can be a positive and preserving force in a child's life. Fears can be useful.

But some fears are useless and debilitating. We want to prevent these fears from forming in our child's heart. If these fears have already formed we want to help our child manage or eliminate them.

Children can have unreasonable fears because of their imagination, which can be so vivid that they have trouble differentiating between it and reality. One way to help a child to deal with these fears is by clearly and kindly exposing truth.

6. A Sound Concept of Self

God values every human being very highly. It is healthy for a child to personalize this truth. A child should personally feel highly valued before God, while not more valued than any other person.

When a child makes a mistake, he may feel worthless. This is when he needs the reassurance of his parents' love. Harsh criticism without encouragement and direction will only reaffirm his unwholesome concept of self. Love will help him correct his mistake and go forward.

We cultivate in a child a proper concept of self by helping him understand his value before God, by helping him accept the fact that he is not perfect, and by helping him be the unique person that God created him to be.

7. A Sound Concept of Others

We should help our child have a sound concept of others. The parent who criticizes his/her spouse, pastor, neighbor, and coworker, is destabilizing his children by destroying in them a proper concept of others.

Our children should have the privilege of growing up in a home where the parents love each other, appreciate other people's strengths, and respect everyone. A sound concept of others is paramount to our child's emotional needs.

Conclusion

Jesus took young children up in His arms, put His hands on them, and blessed them. They knew that Jesus loved them and valued them. Jesus wants to take *our* children up in His arms, put His hands on them, and bless them. He wants to do this *through us*.

How is it with our children? Are they receiving from us the blessing that Jesus wants to give them through us?

A Mom in Training continued from page 9

lived all at once. But rather one moment at a time.

I find that praise goes a long way in training. When I thank my children for a job done right, they strive to please me more. What if I set aside ten minutes—*ten minutes!*—each night before bed, and clear the countertops while my children pick up toys? Do it for one week. When I do this, I am strict. After they are done, I check over their work. I don't tolerate toys in the book tote, nor books in the toy tote. I will call them back out and make them fix it. A few more times and they don't even attempt to put them in the wrong place. They know that Mommy is going to make them come back to fix it. As an example for them, I ask; "What if you wanted a spoon or plate, but didn't know where to look for one?"

"But the spoons are always in the spoon drawer," my four-year-old stated matter-of-factly.

"Yes, because Mommy always puts them where they belong," I told her. "But what if I would just open any door or drawer and toss them in however, wherever?"

"It would be a mess!" she exclaimed, wide-eyed.

"Exactly." That was all I needed to say. Children understand and comprehend far more than we give them credit for.

I am not a harsh mom. I am not an "always-after-my-children-to-fix-this" mom, and I am not a perfect mom I am just a normal, everyday mom. I am a **mom in training!**

The Perfect Cake

ANONYMOUS

"Do you know what tomorrow is?" Cindy asked as she spooned peas on her plate and passed on the serving bowl.

Dennis reached for the bowl of peas. "Let's see, tomorrow is October 5. I think the vet is coming." The peas drizzled off the spoon on a great green mound on his plate. He put the bowl back in the center of the table and looked at his wife, the edges of his mouth twitching just a bit. "But I doubt that's what you were referring to."

"You're doubting right." Flinging a quick grin his way, Cindy turned toward the high chair.

"Here, Jason. See the peas? Use your monkey spoon to eat the peas. Like this—we take the spoon in our hands, shovel on some peas, and eat them." Cindy guided the spoon with the monkey on the handle to Jason's mouth. "Does Daddy really forget what tomorrow is? You tell him it's your birthday!" She dropped the spoon back on Jason's plate and turned toward her own.

"Your birthday!" Dennis sounded very surprised.

Jason giggled at Daddy's wide eyes and uplifted eyebrows. He banged his spoon on the high chair tray. "La, la, la," he prattled needing to say something too. Then he saw the peas in his plate. The monkey spoon stayed where it landed; Jason's fingers worked quite well for peas.

Cindy shook her head. "Jason, you forgot your spoon." Again the maternal hand guided the spoon with the monkey on the handle on its upward journey. "Do you know what a birthday cake is?" she asked her son. Jason just looked at her.

"I'm planning to make him an a-i-r-p-l-a-n-e cake," Cindy told Dennis. "I already have the cake baked. This afternoon while he's napping, I'm hoping to decorate it."

"Cake ought to taste much better in that shape," Dennis commented. "Just don't put too much frosting on it. That'll ruin it for sure."

"That's what *you* think," Cindy retorted, her blue eyes twinkling at him. "Yes, I'll try to keep that in mind. Oh, Jason, that's not what fingers are for. Here, use your monkey spoon."

Dennis watched the spoon scoop potatoes and head into the toddler's mouth. "How old are you going to be, Jason?" As his son's brown eyes looked up into his face, he went on. "You're going to be two years old." Dennis took Jason's hand in his and raised two fingers. "That means you're getting bigger."

"And big boys eat with their spoon," Cindy added. The monkey spoon came with a load of meatloaf for Jason. "Here, Jason, now you try it." She helped him hold the spoon himself. As soon as she released her fingers, Jason dropped the spoon and scooped the meatloaf up with his fingers.

"Jasooon," Cindy sighed. She looked pleadingly at Dennis and whispered, "What shall I do?"

Dennis whispered back, "Does he have to eat with his spoon?" Dennis speared his own last bite of meatloaf. Without another word, he reached for the monkey spoon, scooped up another bite of Jason's food, and held it out to him. When the bowl was empty, he took off the highchair tray and lifted Jason out. "Go get your bear story for naptime."

"Let me wash his hands." Cindy jumped up for a wet washcloth.

"Here, Jason; just wait. Let Mommy wash your hands," Dennis called.

Hand washing finished, Jason headed off for his bear story. Dennis and Cindy looked at each other. Puzzled, Cindy tried to speak softly and respectfully, "Don't you think he needs to learn to eat with his spoon or what?"

CHILD TRAINING FOR MOTHERS 13

"I'm sorry if I made you feel like I contradicted your desires, dear," Dennis said, putting his hand on her shoulder. "Of course he needs to learn to eat with his spoon. But I think learning to eat with your spoon is a trait that must develop on its own and is not one that we can force or discipline for."

"An almost two-year-old should be able to eat with his spoon!" Cindy sputtered.

"Who says that?"

"Well, um, the doctor's book I have says that," Cindy replied.

"Maybe most two-year-olds can. But you know by now that Jason's talking is later than some, and yet he walked very young. We have to accept Jason as he is, don't you agree?"

Cindy nodded slowly. "I see your point. Don't you think I should try to teach him at all?"

"I think we should encourage using his spoon, but if he doesn't catch on, I don't think it's time to discipline him for that at this age."

"By the way, where is he?" Cindy asked.

The two walked over to the bookcase. Their son looked up, grinning, as he gave one more scrape that sent the last books on the lower shelf flying to join the heaps on the floor.

"Okay, Jason," Dennis said crouching down on the floor beside his little son. "You made a big mess. Let's quickly pick up these books. Here, you help by giving them to Mommy. Let her put them on the shelf. There now, we're all done. Next time I want you to just get a book, not knock them all down. Which is your story? Daddy needs to go mow hay. Mommy will have to read it to you this time."

"Thanks for your help." Cindy smiled up at her husband. "See you later. Come, Jason, let's read your story."

An hour later, Cindy returned to the kitchen, refreshed from her rest. "Two o'clock. I should have some time to decorate that cake before Jason wakes up," she said to herself. She mixed up the frosting and collected candy. "All set. Now for the fun." Carefully, Cindy cut and arranged the slices as the diagram illustrated to form an airplane shape. White frosting made the white hull. Lifesaver candies formed little round windows. For the final touch, she added a red cherry on the nose of the airplane.

"Wow," she sighed in ecstasy. "I can hardly believe it turned out that nice. It looks just like the picture!"

Gravel crunched on the drive. Honk! Honk! Cindy dashed for the front door to see the box-shaped mail lady's car. She hurried down the walk. "I have a package for you," Lisa, the mail lady called. "It's too big to fit in the mailbox."

"Thank you!" Cindy said. "Are you enjoying the sunshine today?"

"I sure am," Lisa replied. "What are you up to these days?"

"Oh, our little boy turns two tomorrow. I decorated a cake for him today."

"Two? Already? What fun! Okay, I better run along. I hope he has a happy birthday!"

"I hope your day is special too!" Cindy waved as Lisa drove away. Cindy looked down at the package of mail in her hand as she slowly turned toward the house. "This package must be the new books we ordered." She sat down on the step and used a pin to slit open the package.

"Anything for me?" Cindy looked up to see her husband striding across the lawn.

"Where did you come from?"

"From the hay field," Dennis grinned. "I'm done mowing now, so I'd like to rest while it's hot and have a cold drink."

"Sure," Cindy said. "Our new books came in the mail today."

"Great! Let's go inside, and I can look at them while I relax a bit."

The two entered the house. A little boy stood on a chair by the table—the table that held the airplane cake. Ap-

Reliable
LYDIA HESS

"Stop! If you squabble one time more,
We'll park this cart and leave the store."
But do I mean it? Children sense
If I will mete out consequence—
Or no. Have I been genuine
Or have I told a lie again?

parently, this was a crashed airplane. The whole front end with its red-tipped nose had vanished. Like snow-rimmed volcanoes, several gaping black holes of chocolate cake appeared where the Lifesaver windows had been. The airplane's black chocolate innards and white frosting frame peeked from Jason's clenched fists, stuffed his fat cheeks on the inside, and smeared them on the outside. Jason looked up at his parents. He tried to say something around his mouthful of airplane, but it was too difficult.

Cindy's mouth was empty of airplane cake, but she seemed to be having difficulty saying anything either. She covered her face with her hands for a few moments. Finally she said firmly, "Jason, that's a bad boy." She emptied the fat little fists of their airplane load and smacked them soundly. Carrying him over to the sink, she washed his hands. "Mommy made a nice cake. You aren't supposed to dig into it. That's a bad, bad boy," she scolded. Almost trembling, she set her small son on a chair in a far corner of the dining room. "Sit on this chair."

Hurt by the frustration in his mother's voice, Jason began to cry. He turned, wiggled off the chair, and plopped on the floor. He stared at his mother with utter defiance written over his chubby features and glinting from his brown eyes. Cindy looked at Dennis. For several moments there was silence in the kitchen except for Jason's crying. Then Cindy walked over, picked Jason off the floor, disciplined him, and set him back on the chair.

Jason wiggled off again. Cindy disciplined again, then held him on her lap. After a few moments, she said, "Stop crying now, Jason." Soon Jason quieted. "Now I want you to sit on this chair for a few minutes. I'll set the timer."

After setting the timer, Cindy turned to her husband. She took a deep breath. "Why… what…" her voice trailed off. "Did I do something wrong?" she finally asked, her voice low so Jason couldn't hear.

"You're wondering why I didn't do anything." Dennis bowed his head and lowered his voice too. "I was trying to figure out what to do. I guess it's always so hard for me to know when and how to punish a child in an incident like this. Children are going to be curious and want to explore. How is a two-year-old to know that he shouldn't get in the cake when we've never told him before and he probably wouldn't remember if we had?"

"So we shouldn't punish for something unless we've specifically told them they may not do it?"

"No, I don't think so."

"That makes sense," Cindy nodded. "But I do think there could be times that if they do something very serious like going on the road, they could be punished the first time they do it."

"Yes, I think there could be a place for that. But back to the problem before us—I don't think you did it all wrong. It was right to discipline him for getting off the chair. I appreciated the way you held him afterward and also how you made him stop crying."

"I guess I felt after having told him to sit there, I shouldn't back down very easily." Cindy paused. "I also had this ideal in mind that when the father is present, he should give the punishment."

"I'm sorry, Cindy. I probably should have. I tend to think that when one parent is doing it, that parent should continue, but I do want to fill my part too."

"This child-training business is certainly not as easy as I thought it would be." Cindy chuckled a bit. "But I'm glad I have you so we can work together on it."

"I'm glad for your help too! We must keep praying about it, because we need God's help most of all. Now what can we do with this cake? It looks like there are a lot of crumbs for me to eat."

"The tail end looks almost intact yet," Cindy observed. "But what can I make with that?"

"How about a whale?"

"A white whale?" Dennis and Cindy laughed together.

The timer rang. "All right, Jason, you can get off now," Dennis said.

Jason ran for his father and began to cry again.

"No, Jason," his daddy said firmly. "That was a bad boy to wiggle off the chair when Mommy put you on it. Now stop crying. Let's watch Mommy fix up this cake." Dennis set Jason on a chair by the table where Cindy was working. "Jason, say, 'Mommy, may I have some crumbs since you won't need them all?'" Dennis made his voice sound high and squeaky.

Cindy pushed a pile of crumbs to the side. She smiled into Jason's eyes. "Sure, Jason, you can have some crumbs. See, Mommy is going to make a whale out of this cake. A white whale. How does that sound?"

Jason grinned around his mouthful of cake crumbs.

TO TRAIN Up a Child

ANONYMOUS

When it comes to child training, I did not feel like the stereotypical, teenage know-it-all.

While I was blessed to grow up in a Christian home, my childhood was far from carefree. My dad was a businessman, owning businesses that stretched across several states. He was frequently absent, and when home, was more often than not caught up in bookwork, making him short-tempered and easily angered. My mother was by nature a loving woman, but her less-than-ideal position of serving as both Mom and Dad stressed her to the point of a near breakdown. Often my parents didn't take time to discipline until frustration had gotten the best of them, with the results being that I did not go away from discipline sessions feeling submissive, loved, or repentant. I observed a similar dysfunction in the homes of peers as well, and soon felt disillusioned about the biblical methods of child training.

With this groundwork, I began analyzing child-training methods in other homes. I recall as a young teen, standing outside the closed door of the supply closet at church, shaking in indignation while counting the whacks a young child was receiving inside. My siblings and I had known what it was like to receive forty or more at a session, and I remembered well the trapped, helpless feeling. It was all I could do to keep silent. When a father took a child out during church, I watched the face of the mother. Did she feel desperation at what was happening to her child? I listened to see if I could hear the discipline, and when the father returned, I looked to see how the child was responding. I worked in several homes as a hired girl, and I am thankful that those parents were ignorant of the way I snatched up every detail of their child training and held it under the magnifying glass of my past. Thank God that the mothers I worked for were godly ones, raising their children in a loving, stable atmosphere. Many times I marveled that so little discipline could do so much good. Why hadn't it been that way for us, growing up? What would it have been like to have wrongdoing discussed before punishment, to feel the comfort of a parent's lap afterward? I became obsessed with these questions, driven to the point of inflicting physical pain upon myself at times. This left me even more confused, terrified of the person I was becoming.

Suffice it to say, I was petrified of raising my own children. I did not know how I could trust myself to rightly train a child, let alone trust my husband far enough to allow my children to be at his mercy.

On our honeymoon, I cried buckets of tears; healing tears such as I had never felt before and didn't know were there. My husband held me, let me cry, and said little. My childhood diaries, stacked there beside us on the love seat, told the story.

When a wee baby girl joined us three years into marriage, the fears and inhibitions I thought I had dealt with on our honeymoon rushed back. The intensity of my love frightened me, and I felt overwhelmed by my drive to protect this child. And always, that question haunted my thoughts: how shall we order this child? Is it possible to raise children to noble, Christian adulthood while maintaining a constructive relationship with them?

Baby Lucy grew and waxed strong, and when the time came to discipline, I did not feel ready for it. More healing tears fell as I experienced the special, God-ordained bond between a child and parent when discipline is administered in love. A gaping place within me knit together as I observed my husband lovingly but firmly directing and disciplining our daughter. Who would have guessed that she would love her daddy so, that she would toddle back to the kitchen after a spanking, holding his hand and smiling? Who would have guessed that it only took a few good whacks, instead of dozens? It was almost more than I could grasp.

Enter the maid.

Our third child was on the way when Mary came to work for me two days a week. Frail with morning sickness and busy with toddlers, I appreciated her help and enjoyed her friendship. Lucy, barely two, was at a difficult stage in her little life, and if there is such a thing as the terrible twos, she had a bad case.

Mary had been working for us for several months when her married sister dropped the bombshell. Mary did not think we were model parents. We let Lucy do what she wanted, and she was a spoiled brat.

That evening I wept brokenly in my husband's arms. Mary had hit a tender spot. I knew that in my fear of scarring my children, I had to work to be consistently firm. But

Mary didn't see it all! She missed many clashes of wills between parent and child. Her days were short, only several hours, and Lucy napped much of that time.

Mary's was the first criticism we had received as parents, and I was unprepared. I became hyper-sensitive, overly concerned that we were doing something catastrophic in our child training, and even more paranoid that I would wound my children out of reaction. If Mary said I was not a good mom, she must be right.

Parenting had brought hosts of questions that we had never considered. What do you do when a child doesn't eat? What if she eats only her pickles, and refuses her meat and potatoes? How do you tell whether she is surrendered after discipline? Lucy did not talk at a young age. How much did she comprehend?

Mealtimes became stressful as we struggled to know how to handle the small things that loomed so big. Lucy was a perfectionist. If Mommy sat at the wrong spot to eat, or Mary forgot to give her a fork, we heard about it. If the hard-boiled egg had a nick in it, or the ketchup bottle was upside down instead of right side up, Lucy let us know. Any food on her plate that touched other food caused cross-contamination, and those bites were not fit to eat. Often, we didn't even know what the trouble was, and if we did, we didn't know how to remedy it. Our efforts to force Lucy to eat resulted in spitting and shivering and disdain for the food before her, sometimes even throwing up. We tried hard to keep peace at mealtimes, especially when Mary was present, knowing how she felt.

One evening we decided it was time for something to change. Lucy must learn to like fried chicken. Putting a small chunk on the plate before her, we told her how "yummy" the chicken was. Lucy shook her head. Daddy put the spoon to her mouth, and she spit and shivered. Finally, casting me a helpless look, Daddy picked her up and took her to the bedroom.

Fifteen minutes later, Lucy wasn't the only one crying, and the chicken was still on the plate. What were we doing wrong?

Finally, I talked to a trusted friend about it. She had raised a dozen children, most of them in their teens or beyond, and they were the model of excellent parent-child relationships. Tearfully, I asked her how they did it. I told her of our struggles with Lucy, and how unsure I was that we were handling things right. Should we force her to eat? What about requiring a hug of submission from her after a spanking? Was it okay to switch punishments if spanking didn't work, but sitting on a chair did? Were we making mealtime and discipline—even love—a negative thing?

The wise woman listened, and when she spoke, her words were few. She advised against making food a discipline issue; eating problems usually take care of themselves with time, she said, and mealtimes should be relaxed and happy. She counseled me to keep discipline sessions as short and positive as possible. We should never feel so set on one method of punishment that we can't try another—as long as we don't throw corporal punishment out the window altogether. Most of all, she encouraged me to forget the remarks that Mary had made about us. "You are doing fine," she said. "Mary is known to be critical. Give her a few years; she hasn't raised any children yet." She looked at Lucy, who played in the sandbox a hundred feet away. "Lucy seems like a secure, happy child to me," she said. "Keep on doing what you are doing." She could not have said anything more comforting; it is the nugget I wish to leave with all parents struggling to do their best.

While marriage and the blessed example of others helped stabilize many of the insecurities of my childhood, I found that it takes much time for healing to take place. Nearly six years into our marriage, I overheard a discipline session between a parent and their small son in another home. I listened in growing horror as the spanking lasted for what seemed to be an eternity. Taken off guard to find myself so upset, I shook uncontrollably the entire drive home, pacing the floors once I arrived, until my husband came home. I told him the story between heaving sobs, and he comforted me as I tried to gain control of my emotions. The stress I felt developed into a severe migraine headache, and I spent several hours on the couch with the house darkened. I was surprised to discover that while my tears brought back memories, they were more for the brokenness of a broken world than for myself. This was another step in the journey to complete healing, another opportunity to turn to the Ultimate Healer. Reminders of the past are not always a bad thing.

Lucy will soon be entering her teen years, and she eats fried chicken willingly and without complaint, as well as everything else that is set before her. She comes to us for her needs, and we love, nurture, and guide her and her sisters as best we know how.

Parenting doesn't have to be something that sends a person into a panic of fear and distress. God gives grace for each moment, and mothering is a joy that I look forward to every day.

Dear Mommy
From Your Baby
ANONYMOUS

Dear Mommy,

Do you remember when you held me for the first time? You and Daddy said I was a miracle and you were thankful to God. When you were checking out all my little fingers and toes, the midwife pointed out my thumbs. There were teeny little callouses there where I had sucked on them. You had smiled and laughed and remarked how special I was. You said I was amazing.

One time, when I was a week old, I sucked on my thumb again. You wanted Daddy to quick come and look. You both smiled. Several weeks later I heard you tell him you were glad that I had sucked my thumb again.

When I was three months old, you heard me cry at night. By the time you were out of bed, I was sucking my thumb and going back to sleep. You said you were glad then too.

After that, I often sucked my thumb. I needed only one feeding at night, and you said it was so easy to rock me to sleep and to lay me down in my bed. You remarked to Daddy that I was easier to care for and more content than my older brother had been.

Do you remember all those months before I was a year old, when you said you were glad you didn't even need to rock me to sleep at church? I just sucked my thumb and fell asleep.

After I was a year old, some people started to tease me when I walked around sucking my thumb. Sometimes you pulled it out of my mouth and told me it was yucky. I could not understand that at all, because always before it was such a comfort to me, and I had known you were glad for me.

The older I got, the worse the teasing became. Some people asked me if I had chocolate milk coming out of my thumb. Others just tried to pull it out of my mouth, like it belonged to them instead of me. My aunts and uncles and cousins and siblings and even you and Dad started teasing me all the time. You said my thumb was dirty and I was a baby, and you laughed at me when my thumbs were clean and the rest of my hands were dirty from playing. That hurt.

The part that was the hardest to understand was that before, you said you were glad that I sucked my thumb, but now you scolded or made fun of me right along with all the others.

Mommy, I wish you would not have let all those people tease me when my thumb was such a comfort to me. I wish you would not have teased me either. It made me feel bad and confused!

I wish you would have said this instead, whenever someone started to tease me, "Please don't tease him. We think he is still young enough that it doesn't matter if he sucks his thumb." I really wish you would have explained to my siblings that for now, thumb sucking is okay and they are not allowed to tease.

I wish you would have picked a time, maybe when I became a certain age, and then told me that now I am a big boy and you want to teach me how to be okay without sucking my thumb. Then you would have trained me. You could have made stop-thumb-sucking day a big deal, like some people do when they throw away their child's pacifier, and given me a new teddy bear or other toy instead. I would have liked if you had smiled and encouraged me whenever I wasn't sucking. There are lots of other things to try too, like that bad-tasting stuff to put on, or special thumb stockings. Or you could even have given me candy if I remembered. You could have told my siblings to help me too. They would kindly tell me that I am a big boy and offer a drink or something to eat until I had learned.

During this time, if other people teased me, I would have liked if you had said, "Yes, we agree that it is time for him to stop. We are training him right now. Please don't tease him, because he is learning."

Mommy, nobody likes being teased and nobody likes feeling bad about something they are doing, especially if it was something that was encouraged before. Thank you, Mommy. I know you will take this letter to heart.

From your big boy baby

Confessions
of an Overreacting Mama...

DARLENE ZIMMERMAN

We were going for a walk—she and I and a toddler in the stroller. It was one of those last nice autumn days, when you feel you have to get out and take advantage of the sunshine. And she asked me a question.

Often when my children ask me a question—especially if I'd rather continue processing my own thoughts instead of anyone else's—I think back some years. Back to when I was the child with the questions.

I remember belting out inquiries to my mom when she was in the middle of writing down her list of things to do, or walking into Daddy's office and expecting an answer for something whether or not he was busy. And sometimes the questions were nonessential; the one-to-one undivided attention felt good.

So I try to answer my children's questions. And as I do, the patience of my parents becomes more and more admirable.

That day when we were walking, I was deep in the corners of my mind, fabricating a letter to someone, besides going over the sewing I wanted to get started on as soon as possible. I also noticed—without really noticing, you know—the sticker the neighbor had applied to the side of his mailbox. It featured a heart-shaped flag that appeared to be waving in the wind. And then my daughter asked, "Mom, why do they have a flag on their mailbox?"

I didn't really want to talk about flags, and I sighed—carefully, so she wouldn't hear me. But my childhood memories came to her rescue again, and I began. "Flags are a sign of patriotism. Do you know what that is?"

She looked at me strangely, and I knew that she didn't. I had known that already, but I wanted to keep the conversation on her level. I went on to explain patriotism—that it means to love your country. I told her that each country has its own flag.

She wondered then, what a country is, and we went over that briefly, before going back to patriotism. She was gathering red and yellow leaves along the side of the road, and admiring the creek we were walking past, and she looked very uninterested in what I was saying. It rather annoyed me—she had asked the question, after all! By now I was into the part of how we can't be patriotic because we are nonresistant. And I asked, "Do you know what nonresistance is?"

She looked up when I stopped talking, and I saw that she hadn't heard my question. I asked again.

She shrugged, and I knew that not only did she not know, she also did not care. But since I considered nonresistance to be even more important than patriotism, I plunged into an explanation. She interrupted me once to show me the extra-large red leaf she had found, but I was determined to finish.

About the time we walked past our mailbox, I did finally finish. She perked up again when I became silent. I was satisfied now that I would not have to harbor any regrets for passing off a child's question, even though I had had to shove it all down her throat. Tried, anyway. I had a nasty feeling that it hadn't penetrated very far. She was eyeing our mailbox though and that cheered me. She would notice that we had no flag sticker on our mailbox, and maybe a bit of what I'd told her would stick.

Then she said, "But I thought you said one time that flags on mailboxes are to tell the mailman there is mail to take."

"Oh. Oh, is that what you meant? Yes, that's what they're for."

Oh, well. Maybe, just maybe, a residue from the concern within this caring, albeit somewhat overly zealous mom will settle onto her memories, and be interpreted as love.

It can happen that way. I know from experience!

Pieces

BETHANY MARTIN

Wednesday morning is not the time to start on Monday's wash, I thought to myself. I lugged a basket down the first set of stairs and stepped into the living room. Pieces everywhere. A Lego set scattered across our lovely area rug. Puzzle pieces. Wooden blocks and little farm setups. A torn book waiting to be taped. And pieces of newspaper everywhere. I remember our oldest son Alex (4) saying to his little brothers, "Let's cut out nice pictures to give to our friends." As I got to the kitchen, my heart started to feel faint. I felt like giving the boys a piece of my mind. Why all the crumbs and pieces of bread and crackers? And two meals' worth of dishes.

As I reached the basement steps I heard the sound of my little boys fighting. "Oh God, help me." (My most common prayer.) As I climbed the basement steps, my faith wanted to shrink. Does God really expect me to train all four of these children and keep the house clean and the endless amount of clothes washed and…?

"Hey, boys." My voice was shaking with emotion. "Come, let's have a little discussion." The older boys caught on that something was wrong and came quickly. "Let's take a little walk through our house and look at our huge mess. Shall we make our house nice and clean again?"

"I'll gladly help you," said Alex. He often says that and I know he gets it from his daddy, which means more to me than he knows.

"Can we have job cards?" Jefferson asked.

I decided it would be a good idea. I sat down and wrote jobs on pieces of paper, while they excitedly crowded around me. Then we folded them and put them in a basket.

Pick up block.
Give everyone a pretze.
Pick up Legos.
Clear the table.
Wash the table.
Sweep under the table.
Give everyone a mint.
Pick up books and put them on the shelf.
Clear the silverware out of the dishwasher.
Feed the kittens.
Clean up toys in the periwinkle room.
Run an errand for Mom.
Hold your little sister for five minutes.
Bring down the upstairs bathroom laundry.

Their brown and blue eyes are sparkling as they open their next piece of paper and bring it for me to read to them. And off they run to start the next job. I often give Gilbert (2) his own little set of cards, written for his level. Of course, they are all hoping for the pretzel or mint job card. So sometimes if the same boy gets all the fun jobs, I will slip another one in. Since our boys seem to have boundless energy, they can work hard for their age and they enjoy it.

"The house is getting a lot cleaner. Isn't it fun to make our house sparkling clean?" I ask them. They agree, and I feel my own spirits lifting.

Teaching boys how to work is not for the faint of heart, I remind myself. The crash of the laundry basket sliding down the stairs, or a glass dish falling to pieces after it slips out of little hands is a very real part of teaching little boys how to work. Same with the dirt they sweep from under the table that doesn't quite make it into the trashcan. But they are learning.

On better days we have a little different set of job cards.
Wash cupboard doors off with baby wipes.
Wash dining room window with vinegar water spray and old t-shirts.
Clean bathroom sinks with baby wipes.
Help mommy bake wild blueberry bread.
Tear up pieces of bread for an egg casserole for supper.

I always need to remind myself, even if they are only washing off fifty percent of the dirt, at least they are happy and not fighting. It is obvious that it makes them feel good about themselves to be able to please me, and it gives them a sense of worth, too. Our boys need that.

When Daddy comes home from work, they are all happy, excited about the jobs they did, and best of all, we can welcome him into a tidy house.

Too Darling to Discipline?

EMELINE FOX

What is more charming than a wee lassie twenty months old? I have a daughter of this age who has her daddy's soulful brown eyes. She captures everyone's heart with her darling little ways. She can sing "Jesus Loves Me" solemnly and irresistibly. She can talk much and will gravely reply "yes" or "o-day" when addressed. She can produce a puff of air from her bitty nose when assailed by a hankie. She can hold a pen properly in her tiny fingers and write Very Important Thoughts with utmost patience and concentration. She can understand everything I say to her.

She can respectfully place her hands in her chubby lap and be quiet while we give thanks for our food. She *can*. She did so with a flourish the first month or so. She stuffed her hands firmly down beneath the highchair tray and squeezed her eyes shut before her sisters were properly situated in their seats. My husband and I shared a delighted smile and quickly shushed everyone else in order to follow suit before she became discouraged.

After a while she lost some of her enthusiasm. I had to remind her repeatedly to put down her hands and be quiet. She would obey sooner or later, but then she decided it wasn't necessary to pray so long and would prop dimpled elbows on her tray while our heads were still bowed.

I should have done It then, but I didn't.

Sometimes when irreverent noises erupted from near my right elbow when I was trying to thank God for the food, I glowered the culprit into submission. Sometimes I assisted wayward hands down where they belonged, none too gently.

Sometimes I ignored her in hopes that she would be inspired to follow our examples. Of course this only inspired her to greater misbehavior, and so I resorted to holding her hands down against her wishes. You can imagine how peacefully effective this was.

But I still didn't do It.

By this time she had a cold, so I had the excuse that she probably didn't feel well. I patiently encouraged, reminded, and scolded. That is, I *acted* patient, while inside I was becoming increasingly frustrated with her, and with myself for pushing off the task I knew I had to do. Her bad attitude had rapidly expanded to include the whole eating thing in general.

Why was I procrastinating?

Because she's little?

Because she's not feeling well?

Because she's so darling?

Because I'm always tired and hungry at the moment this problem manifests itself?

All of the above. And I was also being selfish. God clearly commands parents to discipline. I knew to do good and was not doing it. If I didn't do something about this problem it could mushroom into a much bigger one. I had already learned that it is much easier and better to discipline a twenty-month-old than a four-year-old. It was also time to discipline myself. I hadn't even had the chance to properly thank God for our food in days.

Finally I did It. I snatched the defiant little miss out of her highchair the minute prayer was over. Out we went. I explained again that she must keep her hands down and be quiet while we thank Jesus for our food. I administered her punishment. I cuddled her and talked to her some more. She took it so calmly that I feared I had been too easy on her. We returned to the kitchen to face three pairs of sympathetic eyes and our waiting dinner.

My smallest daughter sat angelically in her highchair and ate her food as if she hadn't had a meal in days.

And the next time we gathered to eat, she was the first one ready, with her hands in her lap. Her eyes squeezed shut until only the tips of her lashes were visible among the crinkles of buttoned eyelids. She didn't make a squeak. She looked as devoutly prayerful as she possibly could with such a round, screwed-up face.

I smiled at my husband in delight as we bowed our heads for prayer. My heart was full of relief and gratitude as I asked God to help me be a good mother. I thanked Him for the gift of motherhood. I thanked Him for helping me.

I almost forgot to thank Him for the food.

Train Up a Child in the Way He Should Go!

NAOMI MAST

When thou saidst, Seek ye my face; my heart said unto thee, Thy face, Lord, will I seek (Psalm 27:8).

Are we seeking His face for guidance, so we can be the example our children need and want? Can they follow us and make it to heaven? Or are we so wrapped up in earthly things like paying our debts. Or making sure our children do all the right things to impress others? Without God as Lord of our life it is not possible to raise godly children.

Children internalize their parents in the first year of life. They soak in how we view and interact with the people around us. They internalize how we handle struggles and stress. They catch on how we respect church leaders, school board, and those around us. Are we griping and complaining about other people? We don't have to tell our children; they have already started to think like us even before they can talk. Mothers, are our responses to our husbands important? Let's lay down our differences in churches, schools, or wherever God has called us to be, and let's embrace the challenges and ask God for wisdom how to respond to them. We are either building God's church or tearing it down. What do we want our children to do?

Godly discipline is so vital in how children will respond later in life. He who spares the rod hates his son, but he who loves him disciplines him *promptly*. We need to deal promptly with disobedience. Prompt discipline trains our children to confess and get rid of their guilt. Warnings prolong their guilt, and it is selfish on our behalf to not take the time to discipline. *If we confess our sins, he is faithful and just to forgive us our sins, and to cleanse us from* all *unrighteousness*. Prompt discipline helps our children grasp this at a very young age. We need to examine our own lives and see what God is revealing to us through our children. Do we have things in our lives that we need to give up? We need to ask God to cleanse us and show us where we need to change, so we can have victory in raising godly children.

Praising our children is very appropriate and necessary. We *do not* wait to praise until they reach perfection. We need to praise them on their level. If we wait for perfection, we will likely never praise. This is very devastating to children, because they feel they can never quite please us. We need to praise them for each milestone. This encourages them to keep on and continue to improve.

Do we require our children to be what it took us years to become? Are we expecting them to be adults when they are still children? We certainly need to teach them to be loving, polite, and respectful. We cannot teach this by talking harshly to them and yelling at them and treating them disrespectfully. Are we treating them as we would like to be treated? Talking quietly and using restraint teaches our children more than we can ever tell them with our loudest voice. Can we love them even if they embarrass us? Or do we degrade them to others in their presence? This is very detrimental to a child.

Speaking with restraint to our children, employing pleasant words, and delighting to understand them are not techniques. They reflect wisdom—wisdom that is found in the fear of the Lord. The qualities that will enable you to speak in helpful ways to your children are spiritual.

Proverbs 22:6: *Train up a child in the way he should go.*

LYDIA HESS

Can I pass faith when my own ways are errant?
To train up a child, first train up the parent.
Attend to the Tutor, condition your senses;
Then practice the wisdom His mercy dispenses.

Light for Tonight

ANONYMOUS

Gretchen wrapped two sets of frigid fingers around her steaming cup of mint/chamomile tea. Mint for flavor, chamomile to calm the raw edges of her mind. Her eyes lingered on the verse she was trying to process, *Train up a child in the way he should go: and when he is old, he will not depart from it.* The verse was trim, concise. Like her living room. She glanced up to approve the smooth afghan and straight pillows. True, she let the children sprawl across the floor with their toys. They snipped paper and ate Teddy Grahams at the little yellow table in the corner. Just yesterday she had even allowed Alex and Regal, the middle boys, to spread corn over the carpet to combine, and she had let Drusilla and Arielle have a real tea party right here on the couch with her. No, she wasn't too rigid to allow her children to be children during the day, but at bedtime everything had to be straightened for morning. It helped to keep her soul and mind tidy, she felt, if she could end and begin her days in a neat room.

Usually, it helped anyway. But this morning…not so much. She took a sip of tea, then set her cup down into the saucer on her lap. The cup and saucer was an expensive set from Lancaster County; Gerald had given it to her twenty-two years ago, on her nineteenth birthday. With her fingers, she traced the neat row of spring violets that marched around the cup, then she blew absentmindedly on her tea. *How is it,* she wondered, *that water is shapeless and yet it makes a dip when I blow it?* She blew again, just to watch the mini tidal wave. But then she stopped doing it. There was no reason she should create tidal waves. She wondered how Gerald was faring with this early morning visit to school.

Gretchen got up and put another piece of wood in the fireplace. She could drink her tea in the electric-heated kitchen, but she liked the slow warming of the open fire. Sometimes, when he was not at a scheduled meeting with the principal of Oscar Lane, Gerald sat by her on the love seat; she liked the coziness of that, too. She pulled her mind away from the school meeting and looked back at her Bible.

Train up a child. She remembered a day when the verse had thrilled her, back when Elliot was several months old. Every time he grabbed her glasses off her face, she flicked his cute little fingers, until eventually he quit grabbing.

"Look!" she had told Gerald in excitement. "I trained him to keep his fingers off my glasses."

Gerald had grinned. "You trained him up, and when he's old he'll never touch your glasses."

It was satisfying and rewarding to train a child back then, before Elliot was a year old, when his parents had recently left their teens. Now Elliot was the grand age of fifteen, George was twelve, and the rest of the siblings scattered every two years down to baby Annabelle. Now Gretchen and Gerald were forty and tired. Now child training wasn't really satisfying and no rewards were in sight.

Gretchen remembered a day when a call from Leon of Oscar Lane would have been a request for Gerald to have a school devotional. Not so anymore. Not so last night. How did Leon expect them to get any sleep, she wondered, calling at 9:00 and asking Gerald to stop at school before he went to work this morning?

"Elliot was involved in damaging school property," Leon had said. "I'd like for you to stop and take a look at it."

Gerald had been surprised, and when Gretchen asked,

CHILD TRAINING FOR MOTHERS 23

"*But* what *did he damage?*" Gerald said, "I was too stunned to ask."

Gretchen wondered if any other parents ever looked at each other like she and Gerald had looked last night. "I wish you would be home more," Gretchen had said. She didn't think it was an accusation, but then Gerald said, "I wish you would be more consistent when I am not home," and *that* felt accusing.

Of course, they had gone on to discuss it and apologize and get back on the same page. But still, that didn't erase the fact that Elliot—their son Elliot—had damaged school property. After all their efforts to train him up, he was forgetting. But that wasn't all. Last week, Regal had lied straight to her face. When she asked him if he had seen Arielle's doll he made his blue eyes as round and innocent as could be, and said of course he hadn't seen her doll. The truth finally revealed what Gretchen had suspected all along. Regal had hidden the doll under his bed. He was properly punished for lying and seemed remorseful, but still! He had been trained for years that telling a lie was wrong. Why couldn't he remember?

Gretchen got off the couch, checked the fire, and carried her teacup to the sink. She pulled the metal bowl off the third shelf, and measured out flour to make pancakes. Gerald wouldn't have time to stop in for breakfast after his visit, but the boys were always hungry when they came in from mucking out calf kennels. Gerald had said they had to have one kennel finished before they went to school this morning. She should go out and make sure they were all getting along. Usually Elliot and Regal quarreled the whole time they worked. Alex didn't work. He stood and told stories. How to remedy that?

Gretchen added eggs and milk to the flour, thinking that she really should wake the girls. But they were always so grumpy in the morning that she didn't even feel like rousing them. It seemed like all they did was fight after they were up. Gretchen wondered why the Bible made child training sound so simple and concise, when in reality it was plain hard work. And as complex as the batter she was beating.

Gerald didn't have time to call her until his ten-o'clock break at the sawmill. His voice sounded even older and more tired than it had last night. "Elliot carved a smiley face on the basement wall and he clogged the boys' toilet with notebook paper from the office."

"Is that all he did?" Gretchen asked, feeling a guilty relief. She hardly knew what she had been expecting, but certainly something more damaged than a stuffed toilet. "Notebook paper shouldn't be too hard to unclog. After all, I had to unclog a commode full of Legos. Remember?"

"That was at home," Gerald said flatly. "Besides, this commode is stuffed so tight that Leon had to call a plumber. And, how are we going to get that smiley face off the basement wall? It is about six feet tall. Elliot did all this while everyone else had study hall, and he was supposed to be in the basement working on his biology project."

"Oh." The extent of her son's crimes started to sink in.

"I promised to take Elliot over there tonight to start sanding that wall." Gerald's voice came more briskly now. "So don't have the boys start any more calf kennels. After that wall is sanded, we'll have to put on a couple layers of paint. Elliot has his work cut out for him for a while."

"Okay," Gretchen agreed. "But Gerald! What is wrong? I don't think I know a thing about how to train children anymore."

"That makes two of us," Gerald said.

Annabelle was up from her nap and screaming when the four school children burst in the door. "Mom! You know what! Someone made a face on the basement wall!" George shouted.

"It was awful," Regal said. "Whoever do you think would have made such a mess?"

"I think someone broke in last night after we left." That was Alex—always dreaming up mystery stories.

"And we watched the man clean out the *sceptic* system," Drusilla announced.

"You did not!" Regal guffawed.

"Yes, we did so!" Drusilla insisted.

"Nope." Alex joined the argument. "No one at Oscar Lane watched anybody clean out a *sceptic* system."

"Yes, we did!" Drusilla was near tears.

"Stop it, boys," Gretchen commanded above Annabelle's howls. "You know Drusilla means a septic system. Quit arguing and go change your clothes."

Elliot, quiet for a change, was the first one back to the kitchen. He wouldn't meet Gretchen's eyes as he grabbed several cookies. "I guess I'll go start cleaning out another calf pen," he said.

"No, Elliot. Dad is coming home early to take you over to school."

Elliot's dark eyes darted her way. "Why?"

"I think you know why. You have a big job ahead of you on that basement wall. Did you have a reason for doing it?"

"Dunno. School's boring."

The other boys raced into the kitchen and the conversation ended. Elliot started for the door. "You can work at mowing the back yard till Dad gets home," Gretchen told him.

"He says he did it because school is boring," Gretchen said.

Gerald pulled off his socks and stretched his feet. "That's what he told me, too."

"Did you get very far on the wall?"

"It actually went well. Leon helped too, and we have it sanded smooth. I asked off work tomorrow, and I guess we'll go over first thing in the morning and put a coat of paint on it."

"That way it will look better before Monday?"

"Yeah."

"Is Elliot working nicely?"

"Fair. He's embarrassed, that's for sure."

"He ought to be. I still can't figure it out though. Did all our training go out over deaf ears?"

Gretchen looked at Annabelle's relaxed body. One day, Elliot had been small and moldable, too.

"Of course not, Gretchen. Would Elliot be embarrassed if he didn't know better?"

"I hadn't thought of that. But it doesn't seem like any of our training is bearing fruit lately. I mean you should hear the children argue when they get home from school! And remember that lie Regal told last week? And all Alex wants to do is stand around and dream up mystery stories. And it is like pulling teeth to get Drusilla and Arielle interested in doing any kind of work."

Gretchen laid Annabelle gently into her bassinet and then she threw up her hands. "I am about ready to give up! I don't know what to do next."

"I know what you mean. But things always do look worse when we are tired. Let's get some sleep."

Gretchen shifted Annabelle and sat up straighter on the bench. Brother Peter was telling a story about a little boy named Bobby. "Bobby and his father were out in the woods one evening when it began to grow dark. As they started for home, darkness descended. 'I'm scared, Daddy,' whimpered Bobby.

'Oh, but we have the lantern to guide us,' said Father.

'Yes, but it shines only such a little way,' Bobby said.

"'Hold tight to my hand,' said Bobby's father, 'and we will keep following the light of the lantern. Even though it only shines a short way, as we follow it, it will reach all the way home.'"

Brother Peter looked out over the congregation. "As Christian parents," he said, "we feel a dark uncertainty. How shall we guide our children? Why isn't our training bringing immediate results? We have scary imaginations. We imagine our children will forget all our training when they get older. But brothers and sisters, we need the lantern of God's Word to guide us! Psalm 119:105: *Thy word is a lamp unto my feet, and a light unto my path*. We must have a grip on our Father's hand as little Bobby did, and we need to follow the light of God's Word. It only guides a step at a time. God in His wisdom knows it is best for parents not to know the future. The light only reveals what is best for us. We do not need to worry or fret, but rest! God's light will go all the way. There will be grace for each day."

There was more, but Annabelle cried then, and Gretchen took her out to feed her. A peace she hadn't felt for a long time was stealing back into her heart. She was eager to hear Gerald's thoughts about Brother Peter's sermon.

"I've been trying too much in my own strength," Gerald admitted that evening after the children were in bed. "I always thought I had child training pretty much figured out. If you do this, these are the results. And when the results aren't what I want, I blame myself. I think it is time to focus more on just doing my best and leaving the results with God."

"My, you make it sound simple!" Gretchen said, smiling at her balding husband.

"No, I didn't say it is simple. It is still terribly complex. That's why we need God's light for every step. And I like how Peter said we need the church to help raise our children. I know Leon has had some good advice already, but

I kind of resented it because I thought I had the answers myself."

"I didn't know you felt that way. I was always glad for other people's input."

"I know. You aren't as proud as I am." It was Gerald's turn to grin. "What part of the sermon meant the most to you?"

"I liked all the thoughts. But especially the part of the light only showing a short way at a time. I guess what frustrates me most often is the fact that I want a concise answer." She looked around her tidy living room. "You know…like I keep house. I want child training to be neat and concise. I want to know that if I do this, the result will be this. I want to know that if I straightened something tonight, tomorrow morning it will still be straight. You know?"

Gerald nodded. "But Brother Peter helped you see that the light only shines for tonight, and you cannot see tomorrow yet. Is that it?"

"Yes. And if I am trusting God and doing my best, His light will reveal the next step when I need it." Gretchen glanced down at the wiggling baby on her lap. "Seems this little miss doesn't want to go to sleep tonight."

"I noticed that. I'm going to make myself a cup of tea. You want one too?"

"Sure. Straight chamomile, if we have any left."

Gerald was back shortly. "Here's your tea. Let me take the baby while you drink it. I don't get many turns with her."

Gretchen chuckled. "You aren't home very often." This time she was sure it wasn't an accusation. Gerald's long hours were just a part of making enough money to raise a family. She knew he wasn't avoiding them on purpose.

But Gerald said, "I know I'm not home enough." He rocked Annabelle gently, willing her little eyelids to drift shut. "I was thinking about that during Peter's sermon. Leon has suggested to me more than once that he thinks it would do our boys good if I was home at least part of the day on Saturdays. I guess that advice would be some of the light God has tried to give me that I've been refusing." Gerald rocked harder. "It's not fair to make you manage everybody six days a week. It's no wonder you have trouble being consistent with all of them."

Gretchen felt a warmth from more than just the tea she was sipping. She looked away from Gerald's face, into the glowing embers in the fireplace. "I understand when you need to work long hours to pay the bills, but I know things would go better if the boys could see you sometimes." She glanced back up at her husband, worry lining her eyes. "Do you think your boss will let you have off Saturday afternoons?"

"I'm not worried," he assured her. "One of the other workers has been wishing for more work, but I was too stubborn to give up those couple hours." He slowed his rocker and peeked under Annabelle's blanket. "She's finally sleeping," he whispered. "I'll go lay her down."

Gretchen took another sip of tea, then blew on it. She smiled to herself as she thought of the tidal waves she had created the other morning. The tea was too low in her cup now to make more than a ripple across the top.

Gerald came back empty armed. "What are you smiling about?" he asked.

Gretchen felt her smile widen. "I was thinking that when we look to God for help and follow the light He gives, then our impossible tidal waves can turn into manageable ripples."

She giggled out loud at his baffled expression. "Give me a minute and I'll explain," she said.

Prayer

MRS JOE GARBER

The best that we can give a child
Is nothing to compare
To what the Lord may do for him;
Therefore, we need more prayer.

So, tired parents, do not cease;
Press in, request and seek;
Your earnest vial availeth much;
God can, though we are weak.

Basics of Godly Discipline

MRS ESCH

When I learned to know Florence, she was a godly young woman who had grown up in a stable Christian home. She spoke of her childhood with gratitude and of her parents with respect. I viewed them with appreciation. Surely they were role models to have raised twelve children who were productive members, not only of vibrant Christian churches, but also of society. When I was later asked to counsel one of her younger sisters, I was surprised to discover that the sister was struggling to forgive her parents for some of the ways they had related to her and disciplined her.

In a discussion with Florence sometime after this, I realized she had similar stories. She shared that she had spent most of her life defending her parents' choices, but gradually she had come to the place where she needed to acknowledge to herself that they had also been human. She repented of the ways she herself had sinned and asked for God's help in forgiving her parents' sins against her and her siblings.

As we talked, we discussed the fact that corporal punishment is a scriptural command, though some would consider any form of it an abuse. As Christ-followers, we draw a line at a different place than the society around us does. But where should the line be? I asked Florence this question: "When does it become abuse?"

"I don't know," she answered. "I don't know." And I can't forget her sadness.

I still view Florence's parents with appreciation, but I now also see them as human. They did well in many areas; they failed in several. In miraculous ways, God has redeemed their mistakes.

God also offers redemption for mine. But I dare not presume upon His mercies. As a single woman, Florence realizes she must practice forgiveness and extend grace and honor toward her parents, whether or not their actions were abusive. As a mother, I carry an extended burden—how will I relate to my own children, observing these things? For days, weeks, months, I asked myself and my husband this question: When does it become abuse?

Frustrated with analyzing the complications of that question, we tried another: What is godly discipline?

Godly discipline is administered in love. We start here. My mother once pointed out that I was favoring one of my children. I knew why: I struggled more to love this daughter than some of the others. I disciplined her less, to keep from disciplining without love. Today, I wish that child had received stricter discipline at a younger age; perhaps we could have avoided some of the conflicts we face now. My solution—trying to correct my failure myself—was unwise. I've learned that a lack of love is not an option; love is a choice informed by communion with the God of Love.

More of my children have gone through stages in which I struggled to love them as I should. There is a solution: Pray for love. Don't work around it by punishing that child more or less severely, depending on your temperament. Pray. And pray some more. Few prayer investments have been as rewarding to me as my prayers for more love.

Yet some parents who believe that they do love their children can still make misguided choices when disciplining their children. What are more measures to consider?

Godly discipline is made possible by a disciplined life. Most of us hope that our children will grow up to be wiser, kinder, better Christians than we have been. But we will only frustrate them and ourselves when we demand obedience and submission, enacting discipline from our own undisciplined hearts and lives. When I learn and exercise self-control in habits such as eating, working, and speaking, I am prepared to use self-control in disciplining my children.

An undisciplined life leads to inconsistent discipline. On Thursday, when Mom is engrossed in a book or a sewing project, the children run wild. On Friday she emerges to shake her house back into order, and punishments rain down all day. The children are bewildered, but make the best of it—they know that tomorrow, when Mom is baking pies for Sunday's potluck, they will be able to jump on the couches, dump out the toy box, and hit their brothers again.

Another aspect of inconsistency in discipline is the use of a wide range of physical punishments. Most physical punishments should be administered firmly and with temperance on the seat of a child's pants. A mother who finds herself pinching her child's arm, slapping his cheek, twisting his ear, or rapping his head, might want to stop and prayerfully consider the level of her own obedience and self-discipline.

Too often discipline methods such as these are used because proper discipline is inconvenient at the moment. Last week I stood by the kitchen counter peeling peaches. My five-year-old daughter, Melissa, sat on the floor, legs extended across the narrow space between cupboards, sulking about something her younger brother Hans had done. Hans walked past, stepping over her legs as he went. Melissa lifted one foot just enough to trip him, and Hans fell on his face. I comforted Hans and scolded Melissa. Hans left my side and turned to go back to the living room. As he passed over Melissa's legs, she lifted her foot again. There was Hans, once more flat on his face. I was incensed at the cruelty; my hands were sticky with peach juice, but my knuckles were free to rap Melissa on the top of her head. Very firmly. Four times: *knock, knock, knock, knock.*

Melissa was devastated—and angry. She stormed away. Her response and my own flood of remorse illustrated how a punishment which comes out of nowhere and arrives at any old place on her body can do more harm than good.

Godly discipline is unselfish. Josiah's grandfather gave him a custom-made toolbox for his fifteenth birthday. Josiah's dad joined him in admiring the gift when it arrived. The toolbox became even more meaningful to the teen when his grandfather died suddenly of a heart attack. A year later, after several warnings against a misdemeanor, which Josiah has now long forgotten, the toolbox was moved from Josiah's bedroom closet to his dad's workshop. There it remains to this day, though Josiah has moved away from home and begun a family of his own.

It's true: Discipline will benefit a parent; a disciplined child brings rest to the home. But when I am about to administer a punishment which benefits me more than my child, I need to reconsider. It shows up in subtle ways—I might tell the children that if they have the house tidy by ten o'clock, we'll take a walk. But two hours later, at ten o'clock, I am exhausted from managing children and the last thing I want to do is take a walk. It's tempting to say that even though the house is tidy, they fought so much that we won't go on a walk after all.

Godly discipline is respectful. On some level, a spanking will always feel humiliating. That is sufficient humiliation. Never exacerbate the humiliation by forcing a child to stand in an unnatural or demeaning position for the spanking, asking her to remove clothing, or administering a punishment or prolonged rebuke in the presence of others. Your child is a person. If your punishment humiliates her as a person, she will not feel the punishment, but the humiliation.

Part of respect involves looking at your children as individuals. Sometimes it feels more efficient to me to treat them as a group—and sometimes I can. But they each have different strengths and challenges, and I must be aware of them, individually, to be able to train them respectfully. One of my daughters gets frustrated when it has been too long since I have talked with her alone. Another is more alert to praise and more devastated by criticism. When I look at my children as individuals, praying for the specific struggles in their lives, they blossom.

Respectful, godly discipline does not deprive a child of basic human rights. Be careful about clapping your hand over your child's mouth to stifle his screams—and restrict his breathing. A child forced to go without supper, or to wake early or work late into the night to fulfil his parents' expectations will be frustrated and resentful without knowing why. Children need love, breath, food, sleep, and time to play.

What about the verse in the Bible that says those who do not work may not eat? Some parents have used this verse as in incentive to deprive their children of regular meals. We need to be careful about using God's admonishment to adults as a justification for the way we relate to children. Yes, we train and discipline them to equip them for the Christian life. We train with an awareness of eternal rewards and punishments. But we don't threaten them with hellfire. Children who are threatened during early training— "those who are disobedient to parents and those who lie will go to hell"—will grow up with a warped sense of God's justice and mercy. Little children are accountable to their parents, not to God.

Likewise, we don't punish teens and adults as though they are children. If you are using the rod on your twelve-year-old, it may indicate that you didn't use it wisely when he was three. That's not his fault. The use of the rod when he's twelve will make his problem—and yours—worse.

The godly parent administers discipline soberly. I particularly remember one incident in which my father was grinning when he approached to tell me I needed a punishment. I was affronted, wounded. Later, when I spoke of it to my sister, she remembered it. My father had just walked past a younger sibling who had cracked a joke. He was still grinning about that sibling's joke; he was not finding pleasure in my punishment, as I had assumed. This simple explanation brought me rest. When the idea of punishment brings a smirk to a parent's face, something is wrong.

Godly discipline is accompanied by words of redemption. Discipline should reconcile and redeem. It will always be accompanied by communication. Twenty-month-old Kurt is not to play in the flower pot. When he does, he is reminded of the rule, and then disciplined, and then he sits on his mom's lap and receives further instruction about the importance of obedience. All day long his mother talks to him, thanking him for his help in cleaning up the floor, praising him for his kindness to his baby sister, telling him that she loves him, touching his hair, holding his hand, surrounding him with love and redemption.

Every time I discipline, I aim for the child to leave with the hope that this is likely to be the last time he will be corrected for this problem. I don't want to discourage them with unattainable perfection, but I want to put hope into their hearts that we are finding victory together. After the punishment is over, the offense is forgiven. I won't say, "I spanked you for this yesterday and the day before and the day before that. When will you remember to stop biting your brother?"

When you punish too harshly, apologize. If you find yourself apologizing for harsh punishment repeatedly, seek counsel.

Godly parents welcome accountability concerning their discipline practices. If the neighbor lady saw a mother spanking her two-year-old, they might report her to the state authorities. That doesn't mean the spanking was wrong or abusive. Sometimes I can be so paranoid about what the neighbors might think of the way I am training my children that I fail to discipline them firmly enough.

A better guide is to consider how Christ sees our labor. Yet even that can be hard to do if your own father was too harsh or too lax, or when Christ is otherwise not clear enough to you to know what might please Him. Until you can know Him more clearly, think of a person—parent, grandparent, or any other teacher—in your church, who exemplifies Christ to you. Imagine how you would feel if that person watched you train your children for a day. Then let that awareness guide your choices. When you fear you have failed, find a person like that in whom to confide and confess, someone to whom you can be accountable.

My burden as a daughter, a mother, and a sister in Christ's kingdom is that today's Anabaptist homes would be godly and joyful; that our children will grow up to be productive members, not only of vibrant Christian churches, but also of society. And that they will be able to raise their own children confidently yet trustfully, without a sorrowful and conflicted view of what godly discipline really means.

Fruit in Season

M W

No question about it, it was hot. Away from the fan life felt unbearable. But the real reason today was uncomfortable had little to do with the heat; my children were not having a good day.

What was wrong with them this morning? It was hot, but that was no excuse for all the tattling. Their daddy was gone for the day. No excuse either, but I desperately wished he were here to help handle this.

A voice broke through the smog of my thoughts. It was something I had been hearing relentlessly all morning. The girls had been swapping off, tattling shamelessly, in tones saturated with whiny-ness. I hadn't been keeping track—it was too horrifying for that—but it wasn't unreasonable to think this was the fiftieth time.

When *Momma* is said sweetly, it's fine; I adore it. But not when it's said like…*this*.

Fleetingly, I longed to let someone else face up to the voice this time, someone who would know what to do about it. It was a cowardly wish, but I was all but defeated. And guilty. How dare I recoil from one of the sweetest names on earth?

Sweet, true, but being Momma wasn't only about cuddles and kisses. It had to do with souls needing guidance.

The reality of this was piercing at times.

I drew a deep breath and turned to face my oldest daughter. Beth's voice dripped with displeasure as she demanded justice. She was firing her complaint at me in hopes I would help her to her vengeful goal.

"Momma, all I did was say I wanted to use the bunny fork for lunch and then Kelly said, no, *she* wants it, and she can't have it because it's not her turn, and can I have it, Momma? Can I?" She finished her breathless ramble, face stormy, fists clenched.

Two greedy little girls. Regardless of whose turn it was, the fork went back into the drawer to wait for another day when Daddy would be home. He had more wisdom than I in matters like this.

Brief minutes passed and I heard it again. Now Kelly was airing her grievances. Her older sister wasn't putting dishes away right and it vexed Kelly's proper ways. She was eager to see Beth set straight, at least scolded soundly. I summoned my daughters and reminded them they were to work together peaceably. No tattling, no bickering. It was wrong and there was no need for this.

Their eyes, blue and vast, bore deeply into mine. They gazed so raptly that I could almost imagine I could see their minds wandering. But of course that was only my imagination. A minute later I knew they hadn't listened to anything I had said.

There came that cry again, the tone enough to make me wince. More finger-pointing and selfishness, their voices a cacophony of spitefulness. This was going to take more than a reprimand.

I administered discipline, then gathered my girls around me. I told them, "God is not pleased with this behavior. He wants you to love each other and be kind." They appeared smitten. Dare I hope?

I went to the laundry, optimistic that things would improve now. I hummed as I plunged laundry into the rinse tub. My mind went to James 1:5: *If any of you lack wisdom, let him ask of God, that giveth to all men liberally…*

I had asked for wisdom many times in my life and I asked each morning. Yet I sure didn't feel wise. I was unsteady on my feet, uncertain of what to do with this disaster that our day was proving to be. And as the day plodded on, it became increasingly apparent how unwise I really was—nothing was improving with my daughters. Everything that happened was only opportunity for more disagreements. Nothing suited them.

I was saddened by the behavior of our little blessings. Even more, I was troubled that I could not help them.

Nothing I did changed them; not discipline, keeping them busy, naps, talks, or praying. No doubt I was to blame for their misbehavior. Sometimes I had rotten attitudes. I could be selfish, and I complained too often and too elaborately. Children pick up on things like that. Guilt joined forces with the other pestering issues.

Grimly we plowed through the day, contention dogging the hours. I cleaned, feverishly throwing belongings away. I knew I might regret it later, but as some women delve into ice cream when under tension, I declutter my house.

The urgency to purge our rooms mounted as the girls played grouchily in the sweltering living room. Their play sounded more like conflict than fun with spats that erupted every few minutes.

I crammed a stack of plastic wash basins into the trash can. They probably wouldn't stay there. Some saner day my husband might rescue them, but right now it was my daughters and I needing rescued—the sooner the better.

I didn't know what to do for my girls anymore. I was dealing with something beyond my wisdom, beyond my strength. My mind whirled in blurry circles, too numb to think in a straight line anymore. This shouldn't be happening, I thought dazedly. Why was I letting my children act this way? I knew better. But I felt helpless. I couldn't remember feeling this desperate before, like the scriptural ways of child training weren't doing a lick of good. I knew it wasn't God who fell short, so it had to be me.

Joe came home at six o'clock sharp. I apologized that there was no supper yet. "I honestly can't think well enough to come up with much, but I know we have some leftovers."

"That's fine," he amiably replied. "Why, what's wrong?"

I gave him a mercifully brief outline of our day. We were sitting in the yard watching the children on their bikes. Baby Luke sat in the grass beside us in shirttails and diaper. He held a cookie in both hands, which he munched like a contented mouse. He was oblivious to the chocolate smearing his mouth and eye as the tiny knee propped under his chin.

"Looking at the girls now, you probably can't believe how I said they were acting," I said. For five minutes, Beth and Kelly had ridden bikes with no quarrels over which direction they should ride around the circle. They hadn't debated over who should ride the pink bike or the green bike. It was sadly astonishing.

"No, I believe you," my husband loyally assured me. I started to say more but decided against it. After all, I certainly didn't want to be guilty of whining or complaining.

I went inside to find supper. As I unearthed lettuce, cheese, and mayo from the crowded fridge my mind tormented me.

So what had I done wrong? Was it even fitting that a Christian mother should have children who behaved unrighteously all day long with no signs of repentance? I had taken the best measures I knew. Why hadn't God aided me when I repeatedly asked for help? It seemed like He hadn't heard me, but I knew that wasn't true. Maybe I hadn't heard *Him*. That was it: I had failed God and my children, and that was why the day hadn't amounted to much more than a mess. A big, big mess.

Later, in the quiet space that follows children being asleep for the night, I asked the questions that were eating me. I was giving Joe a haircut in the middle of the kitchen. We were surrounded by toys and dishes I had overlooked in the commotion of the day.

"You can tell me we had a bad day," I said, swinging the scissors at the disarray. My laugh was mirthless.

Growing earnest, I asked, "So did anything I did or said do any good at all?" I swallowed hard. "Because nothing changed." I waited for his answer. Everything was quiet except for the snipping scissors.

Finally Joe said simply, "It probably did more good than you think." He clutched his collar tighter as a clump of hair slid down his neck. Then he added, "I don't mean today…" His voice trailed off, but my thoughts went on finishing his sentence.

But later, if we're faithful, we'll see results. My heart lunged for the hope I had feared was lost and clutched it to myself in gratitude. I was still convinced I had mishandled our daughters' naughtiness—I'm so far from being the perfect mother—but I had done all I knew to do. Perhaps I had to be content with that.

The next day as I rocked the baby I pondered the day before. I still wanted an answer to my question. Why had there been no fruits reaped in spite of my efforts to deal with the children in a godly fashion? I leaned back and closed my eyes, pleading with God for encouragement for

continued on page 32

Out of the Mouth of Babes

MARY E MARTIN

I grabbed the broom from its spot in the corner cupboard and hastily began to sweep up the after-breakfast crumbs. My thoughts flew as fast as my broom. My husband had an out-of-state preaching assignment this weekend. And I was responsible to get our family ready to go along. Simply put, I needed to have five children ranging in age from one year to eight years ready to go on a nine-hour trip by tomorrow morning. And I needed to have all the paraphernalia that it takes to tote children across several states packed and ready by tonight. So many things to do in such a short time!

"Mommy, would you like a sticker?" Three-year-old Alice's voice broke into my plans. Her bright blue eyes sparkled in anticipation of giving Mommy a gift.

"I have three different kinds." She held up three much-loved and bedraggled stickers for me to see.

"Oh, yes! Just wait till I get finished sweeping up my dirt pile, and then I'll choose." My voice sounded pleased, but my thoughts were still in Kentucky. I must remember to pack enough bibs for all the children to wear for Sunday evening supper; I must not forget my husband's suit coat. And yes, I should get out that little insulated pocketbook I had so that I could carry fresh cold milk for Larry's bottle. What should I do about his bottle for on the way home?

"Mommy! Maybe you would like some mother's hands!" Alice's voice brought me back to the kitchen. She held up a sticker that had a picture of praying hands on it.

Now my startled thoughts were focused on stickers.

"Why do you call those hands mother's hands?" I queried, wondering at her three-year-old logic.

"Well," she stalled a little, "isn't that what mothers do with their hands?"

"Yes, that is what all good mothers do," I responded. "And I think I'll put that sticker right here on the front of my dress to help me to remember to be a good mother today."

Alice's eyes glowed as she looked at the sticker stuck on the front of my dress, and she scampered off to play.

As I returned my broom to its closet, I marveled at the reminder that God had sent to me on this busy, busy day. "Out of the mouth of babes," I murmured. I whispered a plea to God for His guidance in training these babes as I headed to the attic to get the suitcases.

Fruit in Season continued from page 31

my weary soul. I trusted Him not to leave me comfortless. My husband and I had a desire to raise our children in His ways, and He loved these children more than we did. I knew He would help us.

As I rocked and meditated, a verse flooded into my mind.

And let us not be weary in well doing: for in due season we shall reap, if we faint not (Gal. 6:9).

Weary. That was exactly what I was. Discouraged, too. It was disheartening not to see results for my endeavors. But to me this verse was saying, don't give up. Don't grow weary, even if there is nothing to show for your well-doing today. Even if you see no fruit at all, no tiny knobs of green giving hope of a future blackberry pie.

Still keep on with your toiling, your pruning and fertilizing. With time the fruit will come. Go at it courageously, never minding the thorns studding your persistent fingers. Blackberry pie is worth all this; you'd better believe it.

It's worth all the sweat, the toil, and sometimes the tears. It will all gloriously be made up for when you take your first taste of warm blackberries, seeping perfect purple sweetness.

And you'll learn that what you were being told all along is really true:

Fruit in season is always the sweetest.

A Life or Death Matter

MRS G

Lillian plunged the cups into the sudsy water. If she hurried fast enough she could get this whole stack of dishes through the water while the children played in the fresh morning air. Maybe this time there'd be no interruptions and everything could rest in the drainer before the water cooled. Maybe…

A couple years ago Kathryn and Yvonne only ventured out when Lillian went to the mailbox or the garden. Now these two little girls had matured enough to enjoy going out on their own. This window by the sink certainly came in handy for watching and washing, because this spring Jerold's eighteen-month-old legs had joined his sisters in their outdoor adventures. He wasn't the timorous, clinging type his sisters had been at that age. All-boy, explorer, independent described him. His sturdy little legs took him far and wide, farther and wider than safety allowed.

Lillian slid another milky cereal bowl into her water and looked out the window. She couldn't trust Jerold out of her sight for more than thirty seconds. Even indoors, he disappeared upstairs while she had her back turned, or he sat under the table hidden in the folds of the quilt she was marking, experimenting with scissors on the folds of pink and green fabric dangling in front of him.

At this moment, Jerold trotted around the lawn waving a stick. The big porch and lawn were a splendid place for the three children to play—as long as they kept their distance from the road. Jerold had wandered the two hundred feet out there earlier in the week. Lillian hoped he remembered the lesson he had received. She glanced out again. Kathryn squatted beside her brother showing him how to pick dandelions.

Lillian scoured the last of the eggs from the edge of the frying pan and slipped it into the still-warm rinse water. Another look out the window showed Yvonne tickling Jerold's nose with a dandelion. Such entertaining sisters should help to keep him out of danger.

Now for the floor. Lillian swished the broom under the table, pulling out several Cheerios and shriveled peas. She retrieved a rag to scrub away the half dry splat of yogurt. Did other mothers' floors deteriorate to this slovenly condition every half day?

"Mom! Mom! Jerold is on the road. Mom!"

Lillian bolted out the door. Kathryn trailed behind.

Jerold was indeed on the road, reveling in this ideally smooth playground where no stones or tangled tall grass tripped him.

Lillian scooped him into her arms. As soon as they were in the safety of the lane, she stopped and pointed. "No, no. The road is no, no. Jerold must not go on the road."

Jerold listened soberly. The cogs of his memory seemed to be processing the instruction.

Before his little mind had time to slip into another gear, Lillian hurried into the house, away from any neighbor's keen eyes and repeated the "no, no," with a punishment. She hugged the little fellow close and wiped away his tears. "You must stay off the road, son." Then she whispered to herself more than to him. "Your obedience could be a matter of life or death."

Back in the kitchen, Lillian filled Jerold's favorite cup, and while he sipped she grabbed the broom still standing sentinel beside the Cheerio-pea pile and whisked all the debris into the dustpan.

By now, the washer had spun the towels their final round. Now she could join the children outside and get the laundry flapping.

Lillian shook one towel after another and pinned them

continued on page 36

A Plea for *Praise*

MRS HORST

There is a burden on my heart for precious children. Are they hearing words of praise *every day* from Mom and Dad? Do they know that they *can* please you? Or is criticism and scolding followed by punishment all they know?

Some children do require more discipline, but they also require and covet more praise. Children need positive comments from their parents. It can have such a boost on their behavior.

Just imagine if all you ever heard from your spouse was negative. *The cookies were burned, you never have the house clean enough, you don't handle the children properly, you ought to lose some weight, can't you make a pie once, and you really should watch your pennies better.* How depressing and how much harder to put in effort to please!

What power praise can do! A compliment for proper behavior will beget more good behavior. It touches my heart to see my children's eyes shine for a compliment for good behavior. I have noticed their efforts since I needed to punish for improper behavior. My eyes mist and I resolve anew to put forth special effort in praise.

My children deserve to know I appreciate them! I want to take the time to thank them for their efforts in helping me.

I have read a great guideline that said, "Give twice as many positive compliments as criticism." I find that a worthy goal, and a difficult one at times. But oh, the joy in seeing the glow in our children's faces. We hardly understand the far-reaching effects sincere praise will bring.

Discipline is important! Praise will not abolish the need for it. But I believe that if our children feel good about themselves, discipline will have far greater impact.

Praise. Praise. Praise. Look for opportunities to thank them. Seek out moments for praise. It does not take long to give praise, but the words will resonate for years to come in your child's heart. *And a word spoken in due season, how good is it!* (Proverbs 15:23).

I'm joining you in the quest for quality affirmation in our children's lives. It is a worthwhile journey!

And, oh, that someday we and our children can hear the greatest praise of all! "Well done, thou good and faithful servant, enter into the joy of thy Lord!"

Like Mother, Like Daughter

CHARITY MILLER

"Mom, I can pour the oatmeal. May I?" Three-year-old Brianna's voice blared in my ear.

I turned to face my blond-haired daughter who was scrambling onto a chair beside the table where I was mixing granola.

"I pour oatmeal," a learning-to-talk voice echoed as Kaitlyn heaved a chair beside her sister's.

"Chocolate chips! Mmmm!" Brianna's hand dipped into the bag and headed for her mouth.

"Brianna, are your hands clean?" I rescued the bag of chocolates just as the hand returned. "Yes, you may help me, but first you need to put your flip-flops in the basket where they belong and wash your hands."

Lifting Kaitlyn from her chair, I led the way back to the door where the girls had kicked aside their footwear as they entered. Weary of issuing reminders but determined to teach them neatness, I supervised the cleanup.

Back at the table, eager hands grasped measuring cups and spoons as oatmeal, flax seed meal, nuts, and chia seeds were added to the large mixing bowl. The beep of the timer announced that my brownies were baked to perfection. "No touching anything on the table," I warned as I headed to the oven. Setting the pan of brownies onto the counter to cool, I contemplated whether to turn off the oven. I had hoped the granola would be toasting by now, and soon the pizza dough rising on back of the stove would need my attention. However, laundry beckoned from the basement, too. My mind whirled.

"Mom, Kaitlyn's putting the spoons in her mouth."

Kaitlyn's guilty look confirmed the accusation, so I collected the set of purple measuring spoons and dumped them into the sink. "Let's hang out the sheets before we finish in here," I decided and turned the oven off. Brianna chattered as she dug her flip-flops out of the basket. I helped Kaitlyn don hers, and we trundled downstairs.

A wave of humidity greeted us as we stepped outside with the heaping laundry basket. The hum of the weedeater from behind the barn indicated Brian's whereabouts. He usually kept the yard trimmed, for which I was grateful.

"Here, Brianna, let Kaitlyn hold the clothespins, and you can pick some flowers to put in a vase." I settled the dispute that had been breaking out.

"May I pick from the flower bed?" Brianna questioned, clearly wanting to make sure she wasn't getting the worst part of the deal.

"I guess you can pick some of those white flowers and the yellow ones." I showed her the patch of daisies and buttercups. "But leave the others alone."

"Okay." Her curls bounced as she dashed away.

In short order, the sheets had joined the rest of the laundry draped on the line, and we trooped inside with a clutch of flowers. The girls, flip-flops and all, ran for the cupboard where the vases were stored. As I called them back, I wondered, not for the first time, how often this scene would be repeated before they would automatically remember to put their things in the proper place.

I cut and arranged the flowers neatly while Brianna filled a vase with water. Of course, this required drinks all around, so we took a little break. Ignoring the bulging pizza dough and unfinished granola, I suggested, "Shall we take Daddy some water? He's probably hot and thirsty, too."

Out came the flip-flops once more, and we crossed the lawn to the barn where the weeds were being slain. Brian gulped down the icy water and thanked us before revving up the weed-eater again. Feeling glad that I had taken the time to serve him, if only in a small way, I hurried to the house as fast as the little feet following mine could go.

"There's Bella! Let's play on the porch, Kaitlyn," Brianna squealed at the sight of her kitten.

"Play on porch," echoed little sister, toddling off after Brianna and Bella.

I made double time without my helpers in the kitchen. Slapping the pizza dough onto the pan, I slid it into the oven. A few vigorous strokes mixed the granola. I spread it onto several pans, humming to myself. The crunched feeling had gone. Several uninterrupted minutes had caught me up.

On a sweltering day several weeks later, I stood with the weed-eater in hand, glaring at the scraggly edges of the lawn. Keeping weeds in check, like many other things in life, requires faithfulness, and because haying season had taken Brian to the fields, the task was mine. Happy sounds drifted from the porch where the girls were playing with Bella and their dolls. With a bit of luck, I could get this trimming done before any spats arose. "Whirr!" I was off, around the barn and flower beds. I paused to wipe sweat, checked on the little ones, and headed down the side of our long, curving lane, weeds toppling in my wake.

Twenty minutes later, the sight of two small figures walking out the lane brought me to a stop. What were those girls up to now? As they neared, I saw Brianna clasped an orange sippy cup in her hand. She held it up to me. "We brought you a drink, Mama, 'cause you're so warm."

Ahhh! Refreshment. Never before had lukewarm water from a sippy cup brought me such pleasure. As I returned to my weeds, I pondered the power of example. My girls do learn things. They are watching me.

(My sister-in-law, Faith Yoder, who is the mama in this story, related this happening to me.)

A Life or Death Matter continued from page 33

to the line while her mind dwelt on far more serious things. Thoughts of obedience. A life or death matter. Even on this quiet county road, there was no way she would let her son wander out there to play. The risk was too great.

The children scampered toward her, each with a dandelion or a handful. So carefree. She tried to accept bouquets from three small fists all at once and dropped half of them in the transfer. They ran off to find more as Lillian flapped the washer wrinkles out of a purple bath towel and mused further.

Obedience stands as a matter of life or death. Spiritually. Eternally. The responsibility overwhelmed Lillian.

What are we teaching Jerold? she wondered as a blue towel joined the growing row. As parents, their deepest desire was to help him know God and reach heaven. Obedience was essential.

While Jerold stood in the middle of the road, Lillian found it easy to see and enforce obedience promptly, consistently.

But yesterday while she kneaded bread dough, the hamburger sizzled on the stove, and Kathryn called for her to look at her wobbling tower of blocks, it was harder. "No, no, Jerold, don't throw your cup," she had said when she saw the purposeful gleam in Jerold's eyes and his upraised hand. But the blue sippy cup crashed to the floor anyway...

It appeared so small.

But obedience or the lack of it wasn't small now, and Lillian knew she had failed. As his mother she was accountable to help Jerold learn those lessons. Well-taught obedience to simple commands now would smooth the path as he grew.

Lillian knew she dare not let him wander onto the road or through life. The risk was too great. She watched him now as he struggled to climb onto the trike that Kathryn had been riding moments before. Once he managed to perch himself on the seat, his chubby legs lacked a full three inches to reach the pedals. He was so little yet; so dependent. He needed someone to give him consistent teaching and a living example. "By God's grace, I will," she whispered to herself.

Lillian set the empty wash basket on the porch and bent over the lad on the trike. "Hang on," she said while she adjusted him more securely on the too-big seat. "Let's go for a ride."

A Proper View of God

M EBERSOLE

Marie slid the pan of granola into the oven and shut the door. *Maybe this is my chance to work on those inspirational cards in between stirring the granola,* she thought eagerly. She glanced out the window to check on her children and was relieved to see them happily playing with their kittens. *Those kittens are a lifesaver lately. Hopefully they will keep the boys occupied outside for awhile yet,* Marie thought wistfully as she opened the spare bedroom door. Here she had spread all her card-making supplies out on the folding table and shut the door between times. She thrilled at this kind of crafting and relaxed as she cut and arranged, glued and stamped.

The screen door opened. "Mom!" nine-year-old Tyler called.

Marie sighed and glanced at the clock. "What?" She tried to hide her disappointment and weariness. It hadn't even been five minutes. The door slammed and footsteps sounded across the kitchen floor and came back the hall.

Tyler walked into the room. "What are you doing?" He picked up the card Marie was decorating.

"Hey! You didn't wash your hands!" Marie yelped, then modulated her voice to a kinder tone. "What did you want?"

"Oh, sorry," Tyler said, and went to the sink to wash. Marie heard him open the hall closet door. Then bumps and grunts. Her heart sank. Sure enough, Tyler walked into the room carrying a folding chair. "I'm staying in now," he announced.

Uninvited, Marie thought. Oh well, she would make the best of it. "What are your brothers doing?" she asked Tyler.

"Um. Playing with the kittens," Tyler said absentmindedly as he sorted through Marie's special stickers. "I want to make a card for someone. Who can I make a card for?" he asked.

It was time to stir the granola again. For a brief moment, Marie thought of sending Tyler to do it. But no, that would only result in spilled granola most likely. "There's a boy your age whose brother died. You could make a card for him," Marie said as she walked to the kitchen. *A good mother would let her son stir the granola so he learns,* Marie thought guiltily. She shoved the pan back into the oven and returned to her decorating.

"Would this look nice, Mom?" Tyler asked as he held up a picture he had cut out.

"Uh-huh, that would be nice on the front," Marie said distractedly, after a glance at the picture Tyler was waving in front of her face.

"I want to use this picture too, but it's too big," Tyler said, pointing to a combine emptying grain into a grain cart that was hooked to an articulating trac-tractor. The picture would thrill any boy.

Reluctantly, Marie left her own project to help Tyler get his pictures arranged on his card when the screen door slammed. "Mom! Can we play in the sandbox?"

"Yes," Marie answered quickly as she slid into her own chair again. She hoped they would go back outside and not come looking for her.

"MOM!" Footsteps came back the hall.

"I said you may play in the sandbox," Marie replied.

"What are you doing?" four-year-old Brent asked excitedly. "I want to do this too! I need a chair. Where can I sit? Huh? I need a place to si-i-t," he sang out as he bounced beside Marie's chair.

Marie could feel herself tensing. "You may go play in the sandbox," she said eagerly.

CHILD TRAINING FOR MOTHERS 37

"Well, I decided I don't want to anymore. I want to do this right now," Brent declared.

Stifling a sigh, Marie finished arranging the roses on her paper and glued them in place. She would have to pen the verse on later when the table wouldn't be jumping around. Besides, six-year-old Kaden had wandered in to see where his brothers had disappeared, and he wanted to have fun making a card for someone too. Marie got off her chair and gathered her things together. Brent promptly claimed the seat for himself. She felt slightly miffed to see him coloring with her glitter pens, but she didn't say anything.

The granola needed to be stirred again, so Marie left the room. *The boys are happy,* she thought. *How important are specialty pens, anyway? Or would Ryan say it's wasteful to let the boys use them?* She shelved the question in her mind to ask her husband later. After all, he was the one who had bought her the pen set.

"Mom!" Tyler called in a frustrated voice. Marie stepped into the room, not sure she wanted to see what had happened. "The boys are bumping the table. I wish life would be right for once!" A deep sigh tumbled across his tongue.

Marie felt herself cringing and yet wanting to smile. "Tyler," she said calmly, looking into her son's eyes. "Life will never be right. It won't be right until we get to heaven. We must accept life as it comes."

"The boys seem to smell when I'm working at the craft table or wanting to do something to unwind," Marie told her husband in exasperation later that evening. This time of day was the icing on the cake for her as she unloaded into Ryan's patient ears. She related how Tyler wished life would be right for once.

Ryan raised his eyebrows. "Where did he hear that?" he asked with a little grin.

"I never said that," Marie denied innocently. "But I guess he senses I feel that way sometimes," she admitted.

Ryan nodded. "Likely so."

"I keep thinking about the child-training sermon we heard on Sunday," Marie continued, "that how we train our children is how we perceive God to be training us."

"Because you struggle to see God as Someone who is patient and understanding," Ryan stated. They both knew how Marie grappled to feel accepted and loved by God. She felt insignificant and tended to fear God wouldn't love her until she was perfect.

"Too often I hold our children to a high level of perfection and get frustrated with them when they are careless or foolish. If I could better grasp God's patience with me and that He isn't wanting to punish me every time I botch up, I wouldn't be so hard on the children." Marie sighed. Startled, she laughed dryly. "That's another thing," she said. "Tyler has been heaving big sighs lately. Every time I hear it I feel guilty, because I know where he learned it."

Ryan chuckled. "Yeah, more is caught than taught," he said. "I also think about how we train our children is how they will perceive God relating to them in their age of accountability."

"That's scary," Marie said, "to be so responsible."

"Not scary; sobering," Ryan answered. "It's not scary when we're open to God's help."

"And God does want to help us," Marie acknowledged. With a sheepish grin, she added, "He doesn't try to escape to His spare room."

A Fine Line

VIOLET MILLER

Lord, give me grace as a mom
    to be firm but not hard,
    to be diligent but not driven,
    to rest but not be lazy,
    to be beautiful but not vain,
    to be simple but not sloppy,
    to be strong but not tough,
    to be gentle but not weak,
    to be righteous but not smug,
    to be trusting but not gullible,
    to be watchful but not fearful,
    to care but not to fret,
    to love like You love, and
    to walk the narrow way that leads to Life.

From My Heart to Yours:

NANCY STOLTZFUS

Mom, is your heart right with God? Are you in submission to your husband? Is obedience difficult for you? Is there sin in your life that has not been covered by the blood of Jesus? These are important questions, and how we answer them will make a difference in the result of our parenting.

The task of parenting is not something to be taken lightly, because there is a soul within every child that will be somewhere forever. We need God in our lives and we need to cry out to Him for wisdom so many times.

When our children were quite young, I tucked a note into my Bible that stated: "My goal for my children is not only to see them become born-again believers, but to be mature, committed, Spirit-filled Christians." I still have that in my Bible, and it has been a frequent reminder for many years.

Every child is uniquely created, so we cannot raise our family in an assembly-line fashion. God is a creative designer, so our children's needs will be diverse.

Become a student of your child. Study his personality traits, be observant to the strengths and weaknesses in his life. One child may be talkative and will freely express himself. He needs to be taught to think before he speaks. Another child is quiet and needs to learn to communicate.

We must be intentional about parenting and think about our children's future. While much is caught from our example, we need to teach them right from wrong. They need to learn self-control, kindness, and submission. We teach them that it is wrong to lie, because God hates lying lips. It is wrong to take what belongs to another, because that is stealing, and the Bible says, "Thou shalt not steal." As they grow older, we add more to the list and that helps to lay a good foundation for godly living.

Every child is born with a will that is bent on doing wrong. It is the responsibility of parents to redirect that will toward God. Part of that process is done by use of the rod.

Don't wait to discipline your child until "you've had enough" or are exasperated. You will discipline in anger if you wait that long. When your child resists your authority and you do not help him curb that attitude, there will be a seedbed for resentment in your child's heart toward you and in your heart toward the child.

There is so much joy in parenting, but that joy is diminished when the child is allowed to whine, to disobey, and to cry uncontrolled. A child can learn at a very young age to cry softly.

A child does not need to be spanked often, once the initial groundwork is laid. This truth was gleaned at an adult Bible school we attended in our early years of parenting, in a class taught by Lester Miller. This was difficult to digest at first, because that is not what we observed in other families. However, we have become firm believers of that method and it works.

Have your rod ready and in its place, so you can find it at a moment's notice. We prefer to use a round, wooden rod.

Discipline in private. Go into the bedroom and shut the door. Apply three firm strokes with the rod to the padded part of his body. Spank hard enough to make it an event, something a child doesn't want to repeat.

Take the child into your arms and speak lovingly to him. Tell him you love him too much to let him have his own way. Tell him this is what God wants parents to do when children do wrong. You may cry with the child and explain that this hurts you too.

Parents need to be consistent. Our children become confused when we do it one way when we are tired, busy, or just plain lazy, and another way when people are watching or when we are angry. Fix it into your mind that the problem will not go away by itself. Rather, as the child grows older the problem will manifest itself in greater sins.

Do not be afraid of your child. You are the parent and you need to be in command. *Never* allow your child to hit you or to say "no" when he is told to do something. Discipline the child every time that happens, and you will be able to curb it very quickly.

There is such a thing as positive or negative parenting. We can say, "Please be more kind" instead of "Don't be so mean." "Please keep you room neat" instead of "Don't get your room so messy." "Do your work quickly" instead of "Don't be so slow with your job." It may seem like a play of words, but it does create a different attitude.

Do interesting things with your children. Go for walks or bike rides, plan a simple picnic, read books to them, and take time to talk. Listen to their hearts without contradicting or criticizing them. Be a safe place for them to share concerns or fears. Some of our children would come to us and ask for talk time, while others needed to be invited to do so.

As our children grow older, we need to relate to them on a different level. Speak to them as you would to an adult. It may seem awkward at first, but it is helpful in forming a good relationship. Involve them in decision making, and do not be critical of their ideas.

Give words of blessing, praise, and appreciation to your growing children. They need your approval. If it does not come from you, they will seek it elsewhere.

When there are unresolved issues in our own lives, it will greatly hinder closeness or sharing. The chains of sin can be broken by the power of God and the blood of Jesus. Oh, the blessings we experience in family relationships when that happens.

Choose to be in submission to your husband and allow him to carry the weight of family matters. When he is not at home you need to do your part to keep your family under control and not allow things to pile up. When you stay current with issues as they arise, the children will look forward to Daddy's arrival, and he doesn't need to dread coming home to an upside-down household.

You are a wise woman if you have learned to refrain from criticizing your husband, especially in the presence of the children. Someone has said, "Children will obey their mother to the degree that she honors their father."

I have always enjoyed the infant stage in our children's lives and wished to keep them there longer. But as time went on I learned to enjoy the special things in every age. Being a mom to teenagers looked very difficult to me, and I honestly dreaded it. Now I think that's one of the best times, and I love relating to teenagers. God does give us grace for every season of life, and when we ask for wisdom He gives it abundantly.

Our children are older now and most of them are married, but I still enjoy reading child-training books. A few of my favorite ones are: *How to Be Parents of Happy and Obedient Children*, by Roy Lessin. *You and Your Child*, by Charles Swindoll. *Raising Your Child to Love God*, by Andrew Murray.

We continue to experience changes in our lives, and nothing stays the same for very long. Omar and I celebrated our thirty-eighth anniversary this month, and we are still best friends. Seven of our nine children are married. We have twenty-four grandchildren and more coming. I spend a lot of time with the little ones and that is a joy and blessing to my life. Praying for my children and grandchildren by name is important to me.

I am indebted to God for the gift of salvation, for enabling power, for teaching me things I still need to learn, and for the hope of being in heaven with him someday.

No Time to Lose

JOANNA YODER

"Good evening!" I stepped into the entrance, and shrugging off my coat, returned the greeting.

"This is Joanna," Janice explained to her preschool daughters. "She is Willard's special friend."

I added my coat to the growing pile on the table. The relationship Janice conveyed by introducing her guests to her preschool daughters intrigued me.

Willard and I had wedding plans, and while that took all my energy and concentration, I dreamed of sharing life with my beloved, and also the sons and daughters God might grant us.

I wanted my children to share their lives with me. As a young bride, I wondered: When does a relationship start?

"Pray your child into the world," Minister Jay advised.

"Sing to your baby," the pregnancy book said.

The day Alayna was born, I was ecstatic. This was my little girl! I dreamed of sharing the kind of relationship I shared with my own mom.

Maybe Alayna would even have my interests. We would craft cards. We would plant geraniums in the flower beds and arrange iris bouquets. Best yet, she would tell me about friendship issues and her teenage struggles.

I'm learning that I need to start working on our relationship today, if I hope for that kind of relationship in ten years from now. And a relationship is one choice, and then another, and another…

We are discussing the upcoming wedding after church services when I notice Alayna is playing with a songbook. I can embarrass her by reprimanding her in front of everybody, or I can leave the conversation and reprimand her privately. If she doesn't obey, I can slap her hand in public, or I can take her to the mothers' room to deal with the situation.

I am canning tomatoes today. Alayna wants to help, but she slows everything down. I can take time to show her how to wash tomatoes, or I can tell her to go play with her dolls.

We are mixing frozen dessert, and Alayna is stirring the milk mixture. I add flavoring. "Why do you add that?" asks my little shadow.

I can answer, "Just because," or I can explain, "This is vanilla. It will give the dessert a delicious flavor." I can tell her the difference between imitation vanilla and the real kind. I can let her taste the frozen dessert we are making and ask her opinion. Does it need more peanut butter? She is three, and will not know if it has enough peanut butter, but she loves the security it gives her when Mom treats her like a person and not just an annoying question box.

Alayna and Julia giggle as they hold hands and skip across the lawn. We are gathered for our annual church picnic and I am grateful to see Alayna is playing happily with her friends.

Then I spot a little boy, all by himself. I can command Alayna to include Isaac too, or I can explain to her that it makes Isaac sad and Mom sad if we don't include him.

Alayna is playing with my paper dolls. It is the cherished wrinkled ones I keep tucked away for safekeeping.

"You must be very careful," I say, handing her the shoe box.

Minutes later she brings me the pieces of wrinkled Robert. "His legs broke," she explains hesitantly.

She didn't do it on purpose. I can scold her harshly, or I can cheerfully tape him together and let her resume her happy play.

Love to children is spelled T-I-M-E. It takes self-discipline to pause in the never-ending work and spend time with my daughter.

Tell her stories. Go on a picnic. Make popsicles or playdough together. Play tea set with her dolls.

continued on page 49

Holding Her Heart
from Toddler Through Teens

RHODA YODER

Renae had a fair relationship with her mother. She respected her godly example and her forgiving, patient approach to life. But Renae sensed that something was missing.

She went through turbulent days in her youth when she felt lonely and confused and longed for mature direction in her life. She had an oversensitive conscience, often felt inferior, and struggled relating with her peer group. She thought of confiding in her mother, but Mom wasn't the type to promote candid conversation.

One day she came across a piece written for young girls.

"If your relationship with your mother is strained," she read, "chances are, the fault is partly your own. Mothers are not magicians. They don't automatically know what makes their daughter moody. Reach out to your mother. Do your part," the article urged. "If you cherish the thought of a close relationship with your own daughter someday, you must nurture a relationship with your mother now."

Renae was inspired to try. After a Sunday evening hymn singing Renae told her mother, "Marilyn stalled on the song she led last night. I felt so sorry for her that I jumped in to help and I stalled too! Caleb laughed, and I felt this tall." She held her thumb and finger two inches apart.

Mom chuckled sympathetically. "I understand how you feel, but in a year no one will remember the incident except maybe you."

The day after Renae had been to a girls' campout she told her mother, "Sharla brought caramel apple bars for supper and mine were plain zucchini bars. I still have half of mine left, and her container was empty. I was so embarrassed."

Mom looked up from the letter she was writing to Grandma. "Look at it from a positive angle. Now we have a ready-made dessert for dinner."

Renae sensed her mother's pleasure as she shared even in this small way, and the bond between them grew.

I know Renae well. Her real name is Rhoda, and I still have a passion for mother-daughter relationships. That is how an idea was born.

Why not ask the young girls themselves: What do they appreciate or what damages relationships with their mothers? So I sent out a survey. The replies came from a variety of church fellowships, and are honest, revealing, and encouraging. But before we look at what they shared, I would like to lay a simple foundation.

A mother-daughter relationship begins at birth. A bond is formed when your child is welcomed and loved from the start. Upon this foundation we can lay building blocks that will foster healthy relationships with our growing children.

What are a few of those building blocks?

1. Love and accept them exactly how God made them.

When your toddler wakes from her nap, greet her with a smile and spend a few minutes of cuddle time.

As you walk past your first grader, pat her on the head and tell her she's your absolute favorite Alayna.

Play paper dolls with her. Go for a walk together. Show

her how to hang up washcloths. Let her help you knead bread dough.

If you can convey how special your child is to you while she is small, your chance of having a well-adjusted teenager is multiplied.

2. Every child deserves discipline.

Breaking your child's will at a young age saves yourself a lot of heartache later. Trying to reason, distract, or bribe your child into good behavior is a short-term fix, but it leaves a weak foundation that will not withstand the storms of adolescence.

When (not if) an adolescent attacks the loving authority of her parents, she is greatly reassured when they remain firm and confident.

Discipline with a caring heart. Jerking them around, shouting, slapping, or pinching is not loving discipline.

One day when our three oldest girls were small they fussed all afternoon.

"No!" cried Esther. "That doll is mine. Give it to me!"

Whack.

"Ouch! You hit me. My nose is bleeding," yelled Carolyn. "Mom! Mom!"

I marched into the living room, grabbed Esther, and led her to the bedroom as fast as her chubby legs could pump.

"Mom! It wasn't me! I didn't slap!" she yelped desperately.

Now she was trying to lie herself out of a punishment. I spanked her soundly.

Esther cried heartbrokenly, "Mom, it wasn't me."

She was right. When we all calmed down I discovered I had spanked the wrong girl. That day I apologized to my little girl, administered punishment where it belonged, and learned a lesson I never forgot.

3. A child needs ongoing support from parents.

We don't support their bad behavior. But your child needs to know she is an important part of the family. She can count on Dad and Mom to be there for her, to pray for her, to believe in her.

I know of one little girl who told her playmate, "Mom doesn't care where I am as long as I stay out of her hair." She didn't have the loving support of her mother. Today she doesn't belong to any church, and her life is marred with broken relationships.

Having laid a loving, prayerful foundation, let's fast-forward to the teens. I asked five questions on my survey. Some answers have been condensed or edited for clarity, but a lot are in their own words.

1. What are your ideals—something your mother taught you that you especially want to pass on to your child?

- I appreciate my mother's deep faith and her ongoing relationship with God.
- I want to pass on an appreciation for my heritage.
- I hope to be as loving, kind, and patient as my mother strives to be.
- The importance of upholding scriptural values in daily life.
- My mom is so unselfish. I want to follow that example.

A major hurdle in the life of our teens is peer pressure. Even when they beg for leniency, they respect their mothers more when they stay kindly firm. Godly direction and clearly defined boundaries provide the stability they crave. This should give us courage to uphold scriptural principles without wavering. Some girls expressed appreciation for teaching in this area.

- Having our clothes modest and within church guidelines is something I want to pass on to the next generation.
- The importance of being confident in doing what is right instead of going with the flow. I want to teach my children not to be fence-crowders.
- We were taught to wear out the clothing we have and that there is no need to have a whole closet full of Sunday dresses.
- Like my mom, I want to appreciate the beauty in nature and flowers, to read Bible stories to my children, and explain the value of our heritage and upholding church standards. I want to explain *why* we dress modestly. Most of all, to teach the plan of salvation.

These girls are not passive puppets with no independent thought of their own. I know the one girl well and her battle with peer pressure was fierce. Now she is a young married woman who appreciates the values she was taught.

A variety of other answers for this question were submitted. The children of these mothers arise and call them blessed!

- I want to love and respect my husband. Seeing a peaceful relationship between my parents gets the credit for that.

- I want to pass on my mom's optimistic attitude.
- My mom taught us to resist flirting with boys. To fill our place in a quiet way rather than trying to attract attention.
- Mom never allowed self-pity. I used to wish she would pity us more, but now I'm glad she didn't. To focus on others is much more rewarding than dwelling on "poor me."
- I hope my girls can feel the same love and acceptance I got from my parents. There were seven girls in my family and we are all different. I never felt like Mom wishes I was more like one of my sisters.
- The importance of being frugal. I'm glad we didn't always need to have the best in everything. It taught us to be creative in making do with what we have.
- Be friends with all the girls, not only a select few.
- I want to do fun things with my children, not always just doling out jobs.
- Mom taught us that life is not always fair, that working hard is satisfying, the ministry is to be respected, and that other people's property (walls, rooms, furniture) is to be treated gently.
- Just because life isn't ideal doesn't give me the right to be ungrateful.
- Take time to listen and don't be too proud to apologize.
- Showing hospitality. We youth can bring guests home, and there's always room for one more.
- By nature I'm an outgoing person and love to socialize. But sometimes we're asked to decline invitations simply to keep our activities in moderation. I'm thankful Mom teaches us to be keepers at home and submit to household duties instead of living in a social whirl.
- I appreciate that we were taught to help, respect, and obey Dad.
- To stick to a job, to do it right, and to be industrious.
- Don't leave the house in a wreck when you leave home. You never know who will be the next person to enter.
- I'd love to have the same management in running a household as Mom does.

No one said she appreciates being allowed to do or have everything she desires. No one mentioned riches or fame. Nor do they hope to keep their family on top of the social ladder.

What they do appreciate are the old-fashioned values we sometimes despair of being able to teach our youth. It's encouraging to know that deep inside they desire and admire Christian values. And they want to pass those on to the next generation.

2. What is a favorite childhood memory?

- My mom and I washing dishes together.
- Picnics, a trip, sitting around the fire, singing together, and mealtimes. I especially remember a day Mom and we girls worked less, then made cards and ate yummy food.
- When Mom would offer to do my chores when I was sick.
- I like to think of the cold days when Mom fixed a warm snack for us when we came home from school.
- I'll never forget the backyard birthday party just for me when I turned eight. I got nice gifts, plus they made special dishes that I liked.
- Sitting together after a day's work and having wonderful family discussions.
- Helping Mom make Christmas cookies.
- Family sharing times—milking cows, singing, going to the zoo. I especially treasure our discussions, and how Dad

Connected

MRS JOE GARBER

Bound by throes of deepest prayer;
Awed by future leagues of time.
Touched by lullabies and cuddles;
Forged by sentiments that rhyme.

Muffled heart-tone throbs connecting,
Held by closest, tender touch.
Forming bonds of strongest measure...
Mama's grasp and Baby's clutch.

and Mom valued our input. Those talks are at the top of my list.

• Quality time spent with Mom, going on walks, talking one on one, her interest in my life, and her advice.

• The times Mom read aloud to us. We also loved family picnics by the river, close to a covered bridge.

• The stories Mom read to us. There was also that time I was really mad. Mom didn't scold. She cared about how I felt and we talked through our differences.

Little things matter. When our children are grown, family closeness is more treasured than a lavish trip to the Rockies. The time parents read aloud to the children is more special than an expensive new bedroom suite they got for their twentieth birthday. Those things may not always be wrong, but if you can't afford it, or if it isn't your style, your children won't have to feel cheated.

3. What is something you appreciate about your mom?

• Her caring attitude toward us children.

• Knowing whatever I share with Mom will be safe.

• She is always willing to help someone in need. She babysits even if it doesn't fit her schedule, and the mothers never find out it didn't suit.

• Mom's caring support when I went through a breakup.

• She considers my viewpoint even when it doesn't match hers.

• I really appreciate how Mom listens without interruption or criticism. Then she offers advice or rebuke if it is needed.

• She is quick to apologize.

• I admire how Mom lives out her convictions, teaching us there's no need to bow to peer pressure.

• I like the way she sometimes stops working to simply talk and the way she boosts my low self-confidence. She isn't only my mother; she's one of my best friends.

• I like how she always has time to listen, even when she's busy at our store. She also gave up hobbies in order to make our home life go smoother.

• I grew up thinking adults never gossiped. I never heard Mom speak ill of anyone, so why would others?

• Mom appreciates nature, flowers, and a good laugh. I love that about her. She also does so much for others.

• The things I appreciate about Mom are: She takes her turn doing the dirty work. She doesn't shame us in front of visitors. She takes an avid interest in our lives. She watches her weight and teaches us to avoid too much junk food. She taught us to respect authority.

Does this list make you feel like you don't measure up? How do these model moms get to be so perfect?

Remember the question? Every mom has her good points, but she also has her weaknesses. Some of the same girls were also open with that question.

4. Is there something you wish your mother would do differently? What hurts you or simply rubs you the wrong way?

• I'm not a perfectionist like Mom is. I love cooking, but usually end up with a messy kitchen. This bugs Mom, but it also frustrates me when she isn't satisfied with my way of doing it, because that is how I cook best.

• Mom likes things done in a certain way. It really irritates me when I don't do something to her liking and she corrects me. I feel like, "Well, what's the big deal?"

• When she blames me for something I didn't do. Also, she wouldn't need to be cleaning all the time.

• Nothing stings more than giving something your best effort, then having it criticized to pieces. Sometimes I wish I heard more words of acceptance and less of criticism.

Apparently perfectionist moms can be hard to live with. Our married daughter, Joanna, recently said, "You always wanted the glider rocker set at a certain angle after moving it for weekly cleaning, and I never could get it right."

I'm glad she told me. Now I try to praise more and fuss less. (Of course, sometimes I sneak back later to rearrange a rug…)

Mothers have different personalities. Some girls are bothered when Mom isn't neat enough.

• Some minor pet peeves are when she leaves messy diapers lying around, and when she makes soup for supper one evening after the next. I also don't like when she works circles around me. It makes me feel slow and lazy, which I am. Sometimes she could also realize she doesn't always need to have the last word.

• When I was still at home I used to think Mom is too laid-back. It also seemed terrible when she taste-tested food, using the same spoon repeatedly. Now that I'm a mom too, things sure look different. I thought I might be like Mom someday, but I never knew it would be so soon.

• I wish Mom were more optimistic, stop being so worried, and wouldn't be so easily offended.

• My mom is a prompt person. Sunday mornings are unenjoyable for me. Getting ready for church brings that promptness into a bad light.

• I know Mom tries to treat us all same, but it sure rubs me the wrong way if I sense she favors a sibling above me.

• Sometimes Mom is so absentminded. That gets on my nerves.

• When I was younger I used to wish she'd take more interest in my hobbies. I'm creative, and she's practical. Now we've established an understood amount of space for our differences.

• Having a quiet nature, I often wish Mom would take time to ask questions, because it is hard for me to open a subject and share. Mom is a hard worker, which is great, but because of it I sometimes feel neglected.

It is good when girls (some were young married women) are honest enough to share what causes struggles in their relationships.

It gives mothers a chance to do inventory and it reminds us of the bumps in our own youth. But I also appreciated answers from daughters who accepted their mother as she is.

• I think the important thing to learn is to stop wishing your mom would be what she *isn't*, and treasure what she *is*. Sometimes that is a greater gift than what you wished for.

• When I was a young teen I could have found something to say on the subject, but now I can't. I've come a long way in accepting Mom as she is. The older I get, the more I admire her.

5. What is a difficult subject to discuss with your mother?

• I find it difficult to talk about my "a bit wilder friends." Too often I find myself excusing them for whatever reasons.

• When my convictions on adult sports differ from my parents!

• It's easy to talk to Mom on most subjects, but the hardest is about the tensions I feel as the oldest girl, because Mom was the youngest in her family.

• I have a hard time sharing personal struggles, doubts, fears, and dreams. I shrink from exposing myself, because I don't want to be thought of as weird or babyish. (Even though Mom isn't that way at all.)

• My serious struggle with peer pressure.

• My broken courtship experience has been tough to share. I feel like saying, "because she doesn't understand," but realize this probably isn't totally accurate. (Aren't girls a mystery?)

• In my younger teens I didn't like to discuss the facts of life. Why? Because it's an uncomfortable subject for adolescents.

• Talking about boys was tough. How is the best way to relate to them? To open such a subject would indicate a problem, and I was too embarrassed to admit that.

Building good relationships is the work of a lifetime. *For precept must be upon precept, line upon line, here a little, and there a little* (Isaiah 28:10).

Rather than concentrating on perfect performance, may mothers and daughters everywhere focus on God, the Father, the Teacher, the Author of all good relationships. As we live our life in worship and obedience to Him, relationships prosper.

On the Same Side
LYDIA HESS
Micah 4:3

Clashing with your teenage son?
Beat your parent-sword
Into plowshares; work as one—
As able—for the Lord.

Ten Tips for Training Tots and Teens

ANONYMOUS

#1 **Get along with your spouse.** Sometimes I have wondered how it's possible that our children even like us for all the times we have failed to relate to parenting in the best way. I well remember the day it suddenly hit me that at least we are doing one thing right: my husband and I love each other! I read years ago that the best thing a man can do for his children is to love their mother. There is weight in that statement. No matter how nearly perfect a set of parents is, Mom is going to stomp her foot in frustration at the boys occasionally; sometime Dad is going to discipline the wrong child. But children can put up with a few failures if they are able to feel the security of their parents' relationship. (We should be sure to apologize to them when we fail.) When parents have true agape love for each other, that automatically spills over into their relationships with their children. Have you ever seen a man who loved his wife unconditionally yell and scream at his child in uncontrollable anger? I haven't.

#2. Don't be scared of your children. Years ago, Katie remarked, "It makes no sense. Most of the mothers at church are scared of their own children." I agreed that this was nonsensical, to think of a woman twenty-five or thirty years old being scared of a two-year-old. But wait. Wait! I was not guiltless. I cringed to remember and didn't tell Katie about the Sunday our stubborn three-year-old got mad during services. Big as he was, he scooted to the floor and refused to climb back up on the bench. I had to hand our infant to another lady so I could use both hands to drag the howling giant off the floor and outside for correction. Thereafter, when he showed the least signs of a temper tantrum during church, I…got…scared. (There, I admitted it to you.) And after Katie's remark, I realized how many times I held my breath for fear my child would not behave.

That is absurd. Children crave security. If I am afraid during a thunderstorm, my child becomes more fearful. If I am calm and collected, the edge of my child's fear is shaved off as well. In the same way, my child has little radars built inside him that catch my fear that he will not behave, and for some unexplained reason, that signals to him that it's a good time to really act up. *Mom is chewing her fingernails hoping, hoping, hoping that I sit on this bench for five more minutes? Great! I'll pick at the baby and wiggle around and squeak out loud just to make Mom pop a blood vessel. Nine times out of ten, I get that accomplished, too.*

No. Oh. No. Scrap that fear! Often, I've secretly thanked Katie for waking me up. I don't have to fear my child. I am the parent. I am in control. God has made my husband and me responsible to train this child, and so we will do it with His help. And instantly, when I kicked out fear, our children became miniature saints, you wonder? Uh…no. But it helped a lot. Try it. You'll see.

#3. Look your child in the eye. Some mothers do this one naturally; others don't. But stopping and looking at your child makes a world of difference in obedience. We've all seen (or been) the harried mom cramming instructions down Cleophas Laray's sternum, "Run get your shoes and socks; it's time to leave! Don't forget to wash your face, and hey, grab a bib for the baby while you are in the bathroom, and…" Poor Cleophas Laray is as befuddled as his name sounds.

Instead, stop dressing the baby for one minute. Call Cleophas Laray to you. Smile into his face and explain to him that it is time to get ready to go to Grandma's. Give clear, simple instructions: "Wash your face. Get your shoes and socks. Then come back to Mother." If he gets back to you before you are finished with the baby, then you can ask him to fetch the bib; otherwise grab it yourself. I have been astounded at how well this works. I can dash around and throw out orders, and no one seems to obey. But when I stop and look the child in the eye and calmly tell him what to do, many times the results are gratifying. If this doesn't work for you, then maybe it is time to shorten Cleophas Laray's name.

Don't forget to look at your young child while he is telling you about the fat groundhog he saw gobbling the blossoms off your peas, too. And when he is thirteen and tries to explain the way cylinders work, look at him at least part of the time even if you can't comprehend any of it. A child, no matter what age, likes to know he is worth your time. Children feel that worth when you give them your attention. Of course, if we have very talkative children, we cannot look at each one during every story. Just try to pay a bit of special attention to each child at least once a day.

#4. Teach your child to work; give him time to play. You may call me old-school, but I still believe that idleness is the devil's workshop. Whether a child is three or eighteen, if he is not profitably occupied, he is going to get into mischief. Now if you are not running a two hundred-cow dairy or growing twenty acres of produce, you might say, "But what can I get my children to do?" Preschoolers should not be a problem; there are always age-appropriate jobs for them. Sometimes you have to get creative to find jobs for all the school-age children while Dad is at work. And I will agree the more creative you get, the more management it will take from you. But I also maintain that teaching a child to work is beneficial in so many ways.

But…all work and no play does indeed still make Jack a dull boy. The promise that he can ride bike for half an hour after washing all the dinner dishes is good incentive for the second grader. Having some friends over to play volleyball or to make greeting cards is a great thing to look forward to after the teenager helps to turn eleven bushels of apples into sauce. Working with your children as much as possible and giving them little breaks like this makes them feel like partners in the work instead of slaves.

#5. Command submission. Submission simply cannot be overrated. Children must learn to obey. If Carolina gets by with pulling your leg when she is two, be assured she'll be doing it when she is twelve. (Don't forget that she'll be stronger then.) I agree that teenagers bring a whole host of issues, but if they are taught to obey without question when they are two, more than likely they will obey (albeit grudgingly at times) when they are seventeen. A child who has not learned to submit to his parents when he is little will have a terrible time submitting to God and the church as he gets older. I know this tip is tough to carry out, but what do you want? A child of yours to be behind bars when he is grown because he won't even obey civil authority?

#6. Don't compare children with their siblings or friends. This one is so easy for us mothers to do. "Look, Rylan! See how well Truman can write his name. I wish you would write as neatly as he does!" Or, "Lora! Did you see how nice Wanita was to Grandma at the family gathering? She sat with her all through dinner and helped spoon in her food. I wish you'd be kind to Grandma too." Does this make Rylan feel like writing neatly? Of course not. Now besides writing sloppily, Rylan is mad at Truman. And Lora suddenly feels all the more self-conscious around Wanita and Grandma. True, we want Rylan to learn to write neatly, but not *because Truman writes neatly*. We want Lora to be kind to Grandma, because being kind is the right thing to do, whether Wanita is kind or not. This is not to say we can never point out another child's good points and encourage our child in that direction, but we should do it very, very carefully.

#7. Respect your ministry. This one can come out openly or subtly; either way, our children know our attitudes toward the church and her leaders. One time our teenagers came home from a cottage meeting with their feathers sticking straight up in the air. Preacher Amos was in charge, and he had told the boys to stand in one room for the meeting, and the girls in another. Our teenagers were okay with that, except the boys had been in a room that was too small. "We were crammed in there!" our boys claimed. "Why doesn't Amos think? There were only half as many girls as boys. If we could have traded rooms, it would have made so much more sense." Our girls agreed. "And the worst part is, Amos said when we go back next month we have to stand the same way!" The children were jerking their shoes off with mutterings and huffings.

Well. It didn't sound fair. But! These attitudes were all

wrong. My husband said calmly, "Maybe Brother Amos made a mistake, but that isn't your problem. All you have to do is obey. Is standing in that room going to keep you from going to heaven?" A sheepish "no" came from the boys. "Rebellion could, you know?" Nods were seen all around. My husband went on, "What Amos asked you to do may have been what Jerry and Rhonda requested. Did you think about that? We don't always have to know why when we are asked to do something. All we have to do is submit, and we can have peace."

I could almost visually see our children's feathers begin to relax. The next month they cheerfully went to cottage meeting, and the boys stood in that same crammed room without a complaint. I shudder to think of the attitudes our children would have toward Brother Amos to this day had my husband took their side and railed on him. Submission brings rest. Let's teach our children that.

#8. Love each child the same. Haven't we all been disappointed at times to hear, "Oh, he's his mother's little pet. He can get by with anything." And we feel just as sorry for the pet as we do for the rest of the children. Admittedly, at times we find ourselves enjoying being with one child more than another, but we *must* love them all the same. Personalities, temperaments, and circumstances all play a part in the dynamics of our children, making them harder or easier to relate to. One family had a son who gave them trials everywhere, including in the kitchen. Dishes upset, milk pitchers dumped, spaghetti flying across the floor. This son's shoes were always open and his face often dirty. He was quick and willing, but who wanted to work with someone who spilled the ketchup all over your dress when he cleared the table? Today this same fellow's shirttail is tucked in, there is no grease on his elbow at mealtime, and he can clean up the kitchen faster than his sisters. Do you think this miracle would have occurred had his parents made a big deal over how much they hated to work with him? And guess what, by the time that son was more fun to work with, another child was working on his mother's nerves. Welcome to the challenges of unconditional love!

#9. Gain input from others. One set of parents will never have all the answers. It is valuable to look around and see how others are parenting. Ask questions. Accept advice. Sit up and listen to child-training sermons. Read the Bible.

#10. Pray without ceasing. Parenting is difficult whether we have a list of tips or not. The only reason I can give any tips at all is because paper holds still. I am struggling along in the same spinning world that you are, where one plus one doesn't always equal two. We reward Gary for weeding the strawberry patch by letting him play softball with his cousins, only to discover he didn't play fair and used bad language while playing. We genuinely love and respect our ministry from the bottom of our hearts only to hear Clarence saying he wishes he could bang some sense into the preachers' heads. We aren't scared of Rebecca, and we look at her when she spends fifteen minutes explaining a new game they played at school, and we thought we taught her to submit, but then she tells a lie to her schoolteacher. See? Sometimes when we add one plus one in parenting, we end up with a really goofy number like fifty-two, and we wonder *where* that came from. This is the part of parenting that keeps us going back to our knees.

It is very disheartening to know that in spite of our prayers and best efforts, our children could choose to reject God and disregard our teachings. Instead of giving up in discouragement though, we need to keep this verse in mind: *And let us not be weary in well doing: for in due season we shall reap, if we faint not* (Galatians 6:9).

No Time to Lose continued from page 41

Recently daughter Angela joined our family, and it caused the whole relationship issue to rock precariously while we adjusted to the newcomer. It also gives me many opportunities to teach and talk with Alayna.

I can accent every sentence with "Be quiet! You'll wake Angie!" or "Hurry, Angela needs Mama!" Or I can involve her: "Please fetch a clean diaper for Angela." And when she comes running with the diaper, I can praise her by saying, "Thank you! You are a good helper!"

Some days I fail miserably.

Some days with God's help, I make the right choices.

Having a good relationship with my teenage daughters is only a dream…but I can have a good relationship now if I make the right choices today.

Micromanaging Mom
JUDITH KRAYBILL

"I want you to sweep the laundry room. And make sure you do it thoroughly," I add as David swings the broom out of the pantry.

"Yeah," he comments dryly. "That's the third time you told me that."

Oh. I cringe.

Motherhood has a way of revealing who we are. After a decade of mothering, I'm still discovering. I realize that words such as "control freak," "perfectionist," or "micromanager" describe me. Ouch.

The realization grows. I weary of talking so much. So I listen as I give directions.

"Make sure you soak the white shirts before you wash them. And if the towel load is too big, divide it into two loads. Try to switch loads in the washer as soon as it stops so you can finish up before lunch," I tell Janelle as she starts the laundry. "And hang up the dresses right away so they don't get wrinkly."

I peek into the laundry room and see the broom swishing around the washer. "Move the boot trays and sweep under them. Same with the trash can. And make sure you sweep out the corners well, and don't forget under the laundry tub."

When they are finished, I scrutinize every detail. "Did you soak the shirts? Are the dresses on the line?" and "Did you sweep in all the corners? Did you move everything?"

Maybe if I give them a whole catalog of instructions with their jobs, the work will get done *right*. You know, like I do. Maybe if I talk enough, they'll never need to go back and do anything over because they'll do it right…the first time …every time!

Why is it so hard to let go? My children aren't babies anymore. Maybe they don't need a catalog of instructions for jobs that they have done countless times. I enjoy doing my *own* housework—thoroughly. But now it's time to hand the responsibilities over to my children. They need to be allowed to grow up and be individuals.

Yes, they need to learn to do their work well. But somewhere there's a balance between sloppy work and Mom being micromanager. So I try to resist my compulsion to give detailed instructions.

I hand David the garden sprayer filled with fertilizer and simply tell him to spray the garden. I show Janelle which seam to sew next on the nightgown she's making. As she stitches, I tend the soup in the kitchen instead of hovering over her shoulder.

Janelle wants to hang the clean curtains in the guest room before company comes. So I allow her the privilege and don't supervise.

Later, after our company has gone home, I pause as I gather the bed sheets. I step closer to inspect. Why do those curtains look a little strange? Oh, they're hanging *inside out!* I smile and wonder if my sister noticed.

Sometimes letting go is difficult. Sometimes it's embarrassing. But in it, I find freedom. Freedom for my children to be themselves. Freedom to teach, rather than control. Freedom in the knowledge that this is best for them.

Repetition
LYDIA HESS

Tell children once,
Correct them twice;
Repeated stunts
Need more than thrice
Times explanation
To instill
Right principles
And wisdom's will.
Truth whispers on.
And on. And on
When we are gone.

Learning from My Father

FAITH SOMMERS

My dad, Allan Miller, loved God supremely, the church and his family passionately. Structure, order, and discipline guided our home. Love and humor made the journey joyful. He loved to preach about the Christian home. Here are a few of his and Mom's guiding principles.

Every child should be prayed into the world, and daily prayed for by name. Dedicate each newborn baby to God in special prayer.

We're a team. Being part of the family means you always have someone who accepts you, someone to listen, to play and work with, to cry when you leave, and to welcome you home.

It doesn't mean blindly defending each other when concern is shared, but accepting advice and admonition so that we can grow together to glorify God.

Loving to be together, knowing that each member is appreciated and valued, cements the bond. We were not only expected to be there at mealtimes, family devotions, or work projects, we wanted to be. Evenings were family time as much as possible. We might read, write, play, sing, but we did it in the living room, surrounded by the others.

As a team, we work together to build the home. Parents should neither make life too hard nor too easy. Sometimes parents can run the little errands instead of calling on a child; yet a child who learns early to endure hardness—that life is not fair—will be a good soldier (II Timothy 2).

Daily take time to look at, listen to, and speak to each child individually. They notice! Invite them to walk to the mailbox with you, to go with you to the feed store, or help you with a chore. Work alongside your children as often as you can. Show them how to live.

When you give a command, speak the child's name, make sure you look directly at him, and that he understands what you said the first time. It's wrong to punish for an ignored directive unclearly stated, or flung at the child as you rushed through the room.

Don't micromanage their lives, but do be involved. Care about their friends, their books, their worries. When children are small, choose for them—at mealtime, or clothes. Then as they grow, let them make smaller, and eventually larger, choices. They will learn cause and effect, and it will encourage growth. They have good ideas. Be secure in your own worth so you aren't threatened by their suggestions and talents.

Children thrive on loving relationships. Love your spouse, honor authority, love the church.

And ye fathers, provoke not your children to wrath: but bring them up in the nurture and admonition of the Lord (Ephesians 6:4). "Provoke not…" may be belittling or demeaning a child, especially in front of others. If you have a child you consider "Naughty Johnny," he will live up to his reputation. Expect obedience. Respect begets respect.

Dad said "nurture" in this verse directly translated is "spanking." God prepared a place for spanking (the bottom). It should be an event, not a wham-bang flyby. The child should know why he's being punished, and after the punishment, forgiven, with the subject dropped.

Sometimes it takes multiple spankings until the child's attitude/action changes. Break his will, not his spirit. A child with a broken spirit will suffer for years, and need God's help to be restored. A broken will at a young age sets a foundation for obedience and submission when the child grows up.

Even babies can be trained to cry and sit quietly. Hold them tightly when they squirm or give a light smack. It doesn't take long until they know why you're restraining them. Often babies are smarter than their parents. If crying babies in church are always rewarded by a trip to the nursery or a walk outdoors, they soon know that to cry gets them out off the bench.

A punishment, even in an older child, or when a spanking isn't appropriate, should be more uncomfortable and memorable than the fun of the disobedience. Don't take the misbehavior personally. Children are not little Christians.

Once I asked Dad about a problem we had. One child would constantly tease, and the other would scream. His advice? Spank them both. Every time. Spank the one you think is the culprit harder, but spank them both. It worked.

Pouting, whining, arguing, and back talk should never be tolerated. The child is miserable, and often if left to himself, will continue to be so; and worse, it's contagious. If we cried because we wanted to go along to town, we weren't allowed to go the next time either.

The Bible way works. Read the book of Proverbs. It's still applicable today.

So those are the basics of discipline. But do it with love and patience. Never in anger. Anger brings resentment. You didn't have a happy childhood? No frame of reference? Do for your child what you wish someone had done for you.

You say, "Nobody likes my child." His advice, "If you love your neighbor, train your child. A child brought up to be obedient, happy, and polite *will* be liked. A parent naturally loves his child. Your job is to train him so that others will like him too."

In all this, enjoy your child. Love to be with him. Carve out time to read to him, sing, play games with him, even when you'd rather be doing something else. Value him, and let him know you do. Speak your appreciation. And always, keep a sense of humor. The joy of the Lord can make ordinary days delightful.

The goal is to raise a child who can live without you. A stable, Christian home life is the foundation for him to grow, and to explore the world with courage and integrity. You aren't perfect and you won't raise perfect children. God can "fill in the blanks" we leave.

These days are gone so fast. If you cherish your family, and they know it, you will never grow old alone.

Guileless
BABY BOY
RACHEL SCHWARTZ

She had no premonition
    Of this scenario
(He was her guileless baby boy
    Those twenty years ago):
That he out of her nine would choose
    His birthright to forgo,
And deal her loving mother heart
    This dreaded, steady blow.

I tremble as I closely clasp
    Our guileless baby boy,
For soon, so soon he'll be a man
    Who brings us grief or joy.
And so our prayers, our toil and tears,
    This earnest aim employ:
To save his soul from him who seeks
    His pureness to destroy.

For raising worthy men of God
    This age is not ideal.
But wait—there is a power that
    Transcends our lacks or skill.
Oh Lord, give us the urgency,
    The patience to instill.
The only hope for victory:
    Surrendering self's own will.

CHILD TRAINING HAS NO *Coffee Breaks*

MABEL REIFF

Maria measured out the coffee grounds and dumped the water into the coffeepot. She glanced at the clock on the kitchen wall. 5:15 AM. There was still time to finish packing Aaron's lunch before he came downstairs for breakfast. She yawned. Getting up with a baby during the night made this part of the morning a challenge, but the quiet was perfect for sharing a few moments of her oldest teenager's life.

She fried two eggs and glanced at the clock again. *He must have forgotten to set his alarm.* Maria finished the egg sandwich, wrapped it in aluminum foil and laid it on top of his lunch box. *Should I call him?* Her mother-heart wanted to make sure he had the best possible start to his day. No, this was a part of growing up. She'd stick with their rule of allowing him to take the responsibility of being ready on time. Three minutes before his driver came, he thumped down the steps, grabbed his things, and made it out the door as the truck pulled in the lane. Maria was relieved that she didn't need to wake him and tell him his driver was already there. *Please God, give him wisdom to do his work for your glory. Keep him safe.*

Maria's husband, Harlan, clumped down the steps shortly afterward, and they took their coffee out to the porch to watch the world wake up. Maria took a sip from the mug she held in her hand. "What's on your list for today?"

"A bunch of odds and ends that I should do by myself." He swatted at a fly. "Can you use the boys' help?"

Maria nodded. "I'd appreciate help, and they give me a big boost. It's just that by the time I've managed everything to make sure they all do their jobs promptly and properly, I don't get a whole lot done myself. Then the next day I do it again…"

He chuckled. "Raising responsible children is not a once and done deal, I guess."

"True." Maria silently added a prayer. *God, please give me enough energy, wisdom, and love to raise—*

"Mom? I need to go potty." Maria swallowed the last drops of the now-cold coffee. She hastened inside to help two-year-old Jason before it was too late, then called up the stairs to wake the other children. It was nice if they could get dressed and do a few chores before they ate breakfast. Another day had begun.

"I'm not hungry." Calvin belched and picked up his plate of oatmeal to set it in the fridge.

"Say excuse me." Maria made a mental note to put those leftovers at his place for lunch. This way the food wasn't wasted and the child was taught not to overeat. She wiped ten-month-old Matthew's hands and handed him a toy so he wouldn't get too fussy before the rest were allowed to leave the table.

"Milk!" No one moved fast enough for Lucy, so she leaped up to grab the milk pitcher. Her hand hit her cup and a narrow stream of water dribbled across the table.

"Lucy!" Jordan leaped back to avoid a wet lap.

"Well, if you had passed the milk…" Lucy huffed as she yanked open the drawer for a kitchen towel to soak up the water. Maria watched to see whether she got everything. She recalled the day an older mom had told her, "A Mom can't sit for a whole meal. It's jump for this and clean up that." Ten years later, Maria could see why this might be true—unless a mom taught her children that Mom wasn't there to cater to them.

"We should do the pig game again to teach Lucy not to stand up." Jordan rearranged his utensils and glared at his sister. "She's always dumping water on me."

Maria noticed storm clouds gathering on Lucy's face and took over the conversation before Lucy could protest. "There are more people with bad habits. What would we work on?"

"Elbows on the table." Daddy looked at Jonathan who quickly slid his elbows back and tucked his arms closer to his sides.

"Burping." "Standing up to reach for something." "Chewing with our mouths open." "Kicking our neighbor." There were plenty of ideas. Maria smiled. No doubt about it. They knew what proper table manners were.

"So…let's pick three things to work at." Maria looked at Harlan and he nodded. If they did more than three, it would be a challenge to remember them all. Besides, if they worked at a few it seemed the rest fell into place, too.

It was soon settled. A toy pig would sit beside Maria's plate for lunch. If she noticed elbows on the table, belching, or reaching across the table instead of asking for an item, she quietly set the pig at that person's plate. The game went on until the meal was over, and the last person with the pig got to wash the dishes. It was a fun way to remind everyone how to behave at mealtimes without nagging.

After breakfast, Maria assigned each of her helpers a chore. She released Matthew from the confines of the highchair and put Jason on the potty while she wrote work lists. Lucy skipped out the door to start hanging up wash.

"See ya!" The door banged. Maria called a good-by after Jonathan who was on his way to his job of helping a neighboring farmer. *Keep him safe, God. Help him to be a light for You.*

"Can I go to the hardware store with Daddy?" Larry asked. "It's my turn to go along."

Maria looked up and nodded. She noticed Jesse stealthily slipping dirty dishes from the sink into soapy water and hiding a grin.

"Jordan, I beat you!" Jesse wiped his hands on the seat of his pants and turned triumphantly to Maria. "Can I have my list now?"

Jordan put his book down. "Huh?"

"I washed all the dishes that were on the sink. Now you have to do the rest because you were supposed to clear the table."

"Oh. I didn't see that you had started already." Jordan sighed and walked over to the table. Maria knew why he hadn't noticed. Jesse had tried to begin as quietly as possible to avoid catching Jordan's attention. Often it ended in a race, with dishes being washed as fast as they were put on the counter. Maria didn't mind, as long as the dishes were clean. It was better than procrastination.

"Calvin, put dishes away." Maria turned and handed Jesse his list. He glanced over it. "Could we do the penny jar for lawn mowing again?"

That had been two years ago. Maria tried to remember how they had done it as she helped Jason dress again. Oh, yes. Each boy got ten pennies at mowing time. For every skipped spot she had claimed a penny. The rest were put into a jar and saved until the jar was full. The reward was camping at the creek for one night. It was amazing how much neater they could be when they actually wanted to. The benefits were still obvious this summer. *Ah yes, like my dad used to say; let there first be a willing mind.* How to show them to be willing was the challenge.

Calvin leaned against her elbow. "I put the dishes away yesterday," he protested.

"Let me think about the penny jar." Maria looked up and smiled at Jesse. *Fourteen. Three inches taller than I am. Where has the time gone? Have we taught him enough? Please, God. Fill in the gaps of our parenting that we cannot see. Show us areas where we can improve.* She broke from her thoughts and turned to Calvin. "You eat every day, too. Get started."

Larry popped in the door. "I almost thought I'd have to stay at home, but finally I remembered where I put my crocs! See ya!"

Maria waved, glad that he found the footwear. Each of the children had only one pair of crocs. Of course, they also had school shoes and church shoes. But if they misplaced the pair they wanted, they couldn't borrow a pair. Maria sometimes felt hard-hearted to enforce the rule. Some of them had a real challenge to learn to keep their belongings in the proper place.

Jordan was already working at his list. Maria noticed him leave on his bike. *He must be getting milk. But where are the jars?* She started for the door to call after him, but Matthew grabbed her skirt as she passed. She stooped to disentangle his little fingers, and already Jordan was around the corner.

Maria picked up Matthew, rubbed her cheek against his smooth baby skin, and played a few games of patty-cake with him. She tapped his upturned nose and smiled at his giggles. So much of a child's brain development depended on mental and physical interaction. *It's miraculous how much they learn, considering they're only born with enough right brain power to control their heart and lungs.* She marveled. *The rest depends on outward circumstances. Of course, the extent of their abilities also depends on God's plan for the child.*

She settled down on the couch to feed him, with Jason and his usual *Home for a Bunny* book beside her. Matthew started to nurse, then abruptly bit. Maria smacked his cheek gently. "Don't bite." He looked startled, then started to wail. Maria knew he was teething, but he still needed to learn not to bite.

Jason watched in awe. "Matthew must obey."

Maria smiled. "Yes, Matthew must obey. You must obey, too, when Mom says 'come.'" Jason nodded soberly. *Each child learns from watching me teach his siblings.* The magnitude of her daily duty to train each one to become a useful servant of the Lord struck her again. *Give me wisdom, God, and love…*

Maria noticed Calvin standing on a chair staring at the dishes. Such a tiny amount of breakfast dishes. "Calvin, bring the timer over here." She took it from him. "You have five minutes to put those dishes away. Pick up one dish and put it away, then reach for the next one." She patted his back. She wasn't always sure how strict to be with him. Starting even a small job and sticking to it was a real challenge. So was getting dressed. The hardest part was getting his attention. His hearing was okay, but auditory processing was a problem. Often it took several tries or a pat on the shoulder before he responded. And he was going on six already. *God, let me never again presume a child lacks training just by observation. Please let the therapy we're doing be the answer.*

The door banged open and interrupted her thoughts. Jordan dashed into the pantry and reappeared with the milk jars. "I was ready to fill the jars when I saw I didn't have them." He gave her a lopsided grin and went out the door again.

He'll remember that better than if I had yelled after him. Maria smiled to herself. *Maybe.* He hadn't seemed at all perturbed to be going that mile and a half the second time.

"I can't hang up the towels," Lucy whined through the screen at the open sink window.

"I don't listen to whiney words," Maria answered. "Lower your voice and try again."

Lucy repeated her question in a proper tone.

"See what you can do until I'm finished here, then I'll come see how you're getting along." That was her favorite answer when a child encountered a tough job. Most times when she came to check, the child had figured things out on his own. Even Jason, whose trike was bigger than he was, often managed to maneuver his three-wheeler to where he wanted when given the promise that Mom would come check soon. She turned her attention to Jason and his book. When the story was over, Matthew was asleep. The short rest had felt good.

She carried Matthew to his bed. A howl of protest followed her up the stairs. She hurried to lay Matthew in his crib before the noise awoke him. She scurried downstairs in time to see Jason pull Calvin's hair. Calvin hit him on the arm. Jason opened his mouth and bent his head to bite when Maria leaped to pick up Jason and took Calvin's arm to separate them before they did any further damage. She took a deep breath and let it escape through her nose. *I know childish spats are an important part of learning to get along with people, but it would be nice if they'd learn faster.*

"Let's shake hands and say I'm sorry." Maria waited while they obeyed. Calvin had barely squeaked out his apology when he began to laugh. Soon Jason was laughing, too. Maria smiled. Her goal of restoring fellowship had been accomplished. Maria gave each one a hug, kissed each little nose, and the two younger boys ran off to play.

She opened the door to check on Lucy. Sure enough, most of the towels were on the line. They hung a bit lopsided, but they'd dry. "Good job," Maria said, brushing the stray hair back from her only daughter's face. *Are you really seven and such a help already? Thank you for a daughter, Lord, but do I really know how to raise a virtuous woman? Please give me wisdom…*

Back in the kitchen Maria saw it wasn't quite time to start lunch, so she decided to clear a few areas of clutter while the boys were occupied with their jobs. The sewing machine held an assortment of wooden pieces. *I told Jordan yesterday to put them away.* Maria scooped up the whole mess and had just dumped it into the trash can when Jordan came into the kitchen.

He noticed what she had done. "That was my collection," he protested.

Maria nodded. "I know. And *you* know I reminded you yesterday to put it away if you still want it."

"Oh. So I can't get it anymore?"

Maria hesitated. *Should I let him have a second chance? What will that teach him? Maybe I could have him do an extra chore like I would if it were a ball glove or something.* She wanted him to realize it was his responsibility to put away his belongings. "Okay. If you wash the lunch dishes and put this away right now."

"Skip it." He flashed his lopsided grin. "I collected them just in case I got an idea." He waved his list. "I have only two more jobs, but I can't decide which one to do next."

"Grandma always told me to first do the things I don't like to do." *And that advice has stuck with me,* Maria thought.

She ruffled his hair. *Now to pass it on to my children.*

"I was doing that. The things that are left are fun things." He wrinkled up his nose at her.

By the time they sat down for lunch, Maria was delighted with all they had accomplished, and she made sure to tell them so. Harlan had gotten more done than he expected, and he had a few chores for the boys that afternoon after an hour's lunch break.

The afternoon passed just as quickly. That night when she sat down to read their nightly bedtime stories, Calvin picked up the *When to Say No* and the *Yell and Tell* books. "Can you read these again?" he wondered.

"Sure." Maria reached for the books that taught about proper touches and laid them on the couch arm while she read from the Bible story book. The younger ones clustered around her while the older ones read their own books at the kitchen table. By the way they often joined discussions, she knew the teenagers listened to the stories, too. *There will never be a point where I can take a break and say I'm done teaching for the day,* she realized. *Training will never be once and done. It's repeated over and over, every day, every minute.* She found the right page and finished her thoughts before she began to read. *And it's not only done by what we say or do, it's also done by what we read.*

Wisdom Within and Without
LYDIA HESS

God's wisdom speaks within the home
Through parent-acts. When children roam,
His truth still whispers in their ears
Above the chatter of their peers.

The Biblical Recipe for Training Up a Man

II Peter 1:4-8

ANONYMOUS

Whereby are given unto us exceeding great and precious promises: that by these [your children] might be partakers of the divine nature, having escaped the corruption that is in the world through lust.

And besides this, giving all diligence...

Child training is not a walk in the woods on a Sunday afternoon. It is prayer upon prayer, exhortation upon exhortation, encouragement upon encouragement, and rebuke upon rebuke. We may need to punish Arthur for cutting up at church Sunday after Sunday. We may need to comfort and redirect another child's oversensitive conscience night after night. We will need to remind our teenagers of the differences between living for self, versus bearing the cross day after day.

We may need to rebuke the twelve-year-old who tends to be silly, and then turn around and correct the anger of the ten-year-old. One child may be a perfectionist who can never do her work well enough to please herself, and the next child may be so happy-go-lucky and dreamy that he forgets to finish cleaning up his bedroom. Or even worse, he never starts!

This task of mothering is so great that often we struggle "to see the forest for the trees." Let's step back occasionally (beside our husband) and take a second look. Ask his advice for sticky situations. God never intended for a woman to raise her children alone. Even if you lost your husband, ask your father or brother or uncle to help you. Most importantly, don't forget to pray and ask God to help you. Make it your goal to pray for each child's weakest area once a day. And if you fall asleep halfway down the list, start at the bottom and go up the next night. Be strong and brave. Child training is not for the faint of heart.

Add to your faith virtue...

At a very young age, we bundle up Arthur and take him to church. We teach him to lisp the words of "Jesus loves me;" we read to him those grand Bible stories of old. Arthur lives in an environment of love and service. As he dries the dishes for Daddy, his soul basks in the love Daddy has for him and for his mommy. Arthur is learning to return love. From day one, our children's lives are immersed in our faith and this lays a rock foundation for them and us to build on. But this exposure is not enough. So soon, we need to move on to the next step. We need to teach.

We need to teach our children virtue—to be good, to do what is right and proper, to be well-behaved. This involves the whole spectrum of life. We teach Arthur to sit still in church, and after church to answer senior Brother Jonas' question loudly enough for him to hear. We instruct him to tell Grandma, "Thank you," for the birthday gift, and to never pick his nose. At our direction, he learns to gather the eggs without being told twice (or better yet, without being told at all, and he learns the consequences of snitching chocolate chips when no one is looking. He learns that to be kind he needs to stop and comfort two-year-old Henry who fell and bumped his knee, but he also knows it's wrong to raid the Band-Aid box without permission. All this makes up the word *virtue* and sometimes the list is overwhelming to Arthur and his parents alike. But let's not give up. Virtuous children are happy and satisfied children.

Don't neglect the rod of correction. If you spank Arthur today because he pouted and whined instead of picking up the toys, tomorrow you may hear him say, "Today I'm going to pick up the toys without crying." (Or you may not—you might have to work on it for a while.) Notice that God never says how many times you might need to use the rod. Having said that, we need to remember that the rod is most effective alongside love and encouragement. Try to help your child have good responses, instead of just punishing for their wrong deeds. Maybe Arthur doesn't know how to stop whining and crying about picking up toys. After you spank, take him on your lap and have him tell you what he should have done instead of what he did. Tell him you want to hear him singing, "Jesus loves me," as he works. (And tomorrow, help him start singing before he starts to cry.)

Rewards and incentives can be a good thing. But keep them simple and cheap. Burn a candle at the supper table on the day that Arthur kept his name off the board at school. Promise the girls that if they clean up the house in time, you will take them stargazing on an old blanket. Sometimes just take one child at a time—maybe the one who needed the most correction lately.

Try to capitalize on your children's good points. Maybe Arthur is very creative, but also very scatterbrained. Tell him that if he remembers to hang up his jacket for one week, then he may choose part of the supper menu and help to prepare it. We tend to shy away from rewards that take time, but how devoted are we to helping Arthur? Remember that age-old adage, "A child spells love, T-I-M-E." We may need to leave the clean laundry in the basket overnight so we have time to help Arthur prepare the dish he chose—be it Checkerboard Casserole or Double Chocolate Creme Puffs. Arthur won't mind if he needs to wear a wrinkly shirt one day, but he will remember those chocolate creme puffs.

Another thing you can do to inspire virtue is to have a goal that involves everyone. Do you struggle to maintain an orderly, happy environment at mealtime? Set up a simple program to help your children to *want* to do better. Tack a list of rules on the refrigerator. 1. Come promptly to the table when called for mealtime. 2. Keep eyes shut during prayer. 3. No complaining or arguing at the table. 4. Ask permission before getting off your chair. Put a mark behind the rule for every transgression. Promise that at the end of the week you will have a picnic under the tree for Saturday dinner unless you get more than so many marks. Set the number low enough to inspire, yet not so low that it's unattainable.

Be creative in your goals. Children thrive on creativity. I repeat that the rod must be used with love and encouragement. Using too much rod and too little inspiration will result in a good child who is frustrated and discouraged. Squash the bad, but nurture the good.

And to virtue knowledge...

So. Arthur knows how to be good. He closes his eyes during prayer. He knows he shouldn't waste his pennies on Pringles or his dollars on decorations. And he knows it's wrong to speak disrespectfully of church leaders. But does he *really know?*

Does he understand that the reason why he shuts his eyes during prayer is because *he* is talking to God? Or is he merely holding his eyes shut so Daddy can pray? Have we explained the principles of stewardship and contentment clearly enough that he understands why he shouldn't waste his money? Or does he feel like this is just one of Mom's hobby horses? More importantly, do we *live* these principles ourselves so that Arthur has an example of how this works out in daily life?

How does Arthur really perceive the church and her leaders? We live in a culture that promotes self and demotes obedience and submission. This mentality has crept into our churches, and sooner or later Arthur will need to decide what he will do. We need to get these issues resolved in our own lives before our children need answers. Remember this, fellow parents, unless your church is apostatizing, submission and respect take care of a lot of questions in church life. If we as parents are struggling to submit and obey, we can expect that our children will be confused. What do we tell Arthur when he sees something in church life that isn't right? Do we give him the right kind of knowledge—the knowledge that will help him to overcome at crucial times? A few years ago, my widow friend told me, "I have decided that the most important thing I can do to increase my children's stability is to teach them to love and obey their church leaders." (Needless to say, she is a great woman, as the Shunamite of old.)

So, we not only need to teach virtue, doing that which is good and right on the surface, but as our child grows older, we need to work on the inner man. Give him the knowledge that is the core of virtue.

And to knowledge temperance, and to temperance patience,

and to patience godliness, and to godliness brotherly kindness, and to brotherly kindness charity.

When our children are small, we command them to do things. *Brush your teeth. Scrape your plate. Go to bed and be quiet.* But as our children enter the adolescent years, we need to start backing off on the commanding aspect of child training. It is possible to do so much commanding that we crush the personal conviction that is blossoming in our child's soul. We need to step back enough to let God's Spirit take over. We have saturated Arthur's life with our faith. We have commanded and taught him to be virtuous. And we have given him the knowledge of how and why God's ways work best. Now the rest of these ingredients are fruits of the Spirit. They work from the inside out.

We may have the rule that Arthur may only eat three cookies for his after-school snack. But when Arthur decides to skip the cookies because the teacher served chocolate pie at school before dismissal, we can know Arthur is learning the meaning of temperance.

We can tell Arthur that he may not upbraid his little brother for being lazy, but when Arthur voluntarily helps him carry his bucket of feed to the chicken house, then we know he is truly learning patience.

We can pack Arthur off to Bible school for three weeks, but when Arthur comes back home and continues an in-depth study of the Book of John, then we know that Arthur is becoming godly.

We can send Arthur to help a busy farmer fill silo, but when he willingly shovels the rotten silage away from the bottom of the silo chute, it's brotherly kindness at work—from Arthur's heart.

And we can teach him all about love and its mighty out-working, but when we see him turning the other cheek and going the second mile the day an angry neighbor stops by, *then* we can know that Arthur knows what true love is!

For if these things be in you, and abound, they make you that ye shall neither be barren nor unfruitful in the knowledge of our Lord Jesus Christ.

Though we often fail, we continue putting forth our best efforts to give our children the training they need to face life and all its perplexities. But Arthur needs to personally decide to take hold of our faith, virtuously use the knowledge we gave him, and to let the Spirit refine him. Finally, as he lets the Spirit rule his life, Arthur has become a man of God.

Exposi–story
LYDIA HESS

II Samuel 12:1-15

You need no rhythm nor a rhyme
To share your Once Upon a Time;
But in it paint a simple scene
And show the lesson in between.
If Nathan could convict a king,
Your parable can also bring
A well-aimed line, "Thou art the one,"
To reach and teach your erring son.

Moods and Candy Canes

JUDITH KRAYBILL

Sarah sang as she pinned the last pieces of laundry to the line. Such lovely sunshine! Who wouldn't be invigorated with the advent of spring after months of snow and cold? Sarah hadn't gotten an early start with the laundry. And, with such a beautiful day, she'd added a load of bedding to the normal Monday mounds. *With the thermometer showing 48 degrees and a brisk breeze blowing, the laundry should dry before supper even if it's after lunchtime,* she thought.

Her thoughts continued as she walked to the house. *It's so special to have the children home from school for a few days during teachers' meetings. And everyone did their jobs so cheerfully this morning.*

Quarreling voices rudely ended her musings as Sarah opened the door and stepped inside.

"What's going on?" she asked as she entered the kitchen where the girls were doing the dishes.

"Janelle is trying to help me sing the song we learned in Sunday school and she keeps messing me up," Kaylene complained from her dish-washing post.

"Janelle," Sarah addressed her eleven-year-old daughter. "Could you hear that Kaylene didn't want you to help?"

Janelle nodded slightly.

"Well, then I shouldn't need to tell you to stop," Sarah scolded. "You're old enough to know how to be kind."

"And, Janelle," she added as she walked past the table where her daughter's book bag hung from a chair. "You shouldn't hang your book bag when it's full. That's hard on it." Sarah set it on the floor. "Put it away when you're finished washing dishes.

Without a word, Janelle glanced sulkily at her mother.

"Answer me nicely when I talk to you," Sarah instructed.

"Okay," she mumbled and sighed loudly.

Sarah resisted the urge to do the same. "I'm going to call Daddy," she said to the children. "Finish your jobs, then sit in the living room and wait for story time." As Sarah picked up the phone for their normal lunch hour chat, Janelle glared at her. Frustration mounted in Sarah. *That* would be the first subject of discussion.

"What should I do?" Sarah wailed to Nathan a few minutes later, after briefing him on the situation. "It's so frustrating. Does she need more love? A lecture? A punishment?"

"Some of all of the above," Nathan answered calmly. "Do you really have no idea what to do?"

"No, I don't. No one ever told me how to mother an eleven-year-old girl. And she's nearly too big to be spanked."

"You need to be firm with her. Sit down and tell her exactly what's wrong and what she needs to do differently. Then, if she doesn't respond, we'll need to take away some privileges."

"Like what? Last week, she was reading when she should have been working. When I told her no more reading for two days, she acted like she didn't even care."

"That's manipulating. If she can act like that, then she's still winning," Nathan said. "It needs to 'hurt' enough that she gives in. And she'll probably cry about it if she's truly at the end of herself."

Sarah pondered the discussion and their eldest daughter, as she mechanically read stories to the children. Then it was nap time for the two youngest and quiet hour for everyone else.

After quiet hour, Sarah directed the children's jobs.

"David, I'd like to stack the load of wood that Daddy brought home last evening. You start and I'll soon be out to help you. Come, Sharita, do you want to go outside?

"I'd like you to sweep the kitchen floor, please, before you come outside," Sarah instructed Janelle as she helped Sharita into her coat.

Janelle sighed loudly. While Sarah tugged Sharita's boots on, she heard another loud sigh.

"There!" Sarah exclaimed as she pulled a beanie on Sharita's head. "You may go outside with David. Mother needs to talk with Janelle and then I'll come out.

"Janelle, come back to the office," Sarah ordered quietly. She breathed a quick prayer for help as she shut the door.

Janelle plopped down on the rocker in the corner. Sarah sat on the desk chair and studied her daughter.

"We can't have you acting like this," Sarah began. "Either you change your attitude on your own or we'll need to help you change it. Do you want help?"

"No!" Janelle shook her head for emphasis and gazed stonily out the window.

"Is something wrong?" Sarah asked.

Janelle shrugged.

"Are you not feeling well?" Sarah probed, trying to keep her voice gentle when exasperation wanted to spill out.

Another shrug. Some tears.

"Janelle, try to talk to me. I don't know anything when you just shrug your shoulders."

Sarah gazed at her daughter, huddled in the chair. Suddenly a rush of compassion flowed over her and she saw herself huddled on that chair.

Of course, Sarah knew exactly how she felt! She remembered many evenings, crying to Hubby after the children were in bed, wishing to be a better mom, a better wife, a better Christian.

Sarah's tone softened. "Is it hard to be good?"

Janelle nodded.

"Does it feel like you do everything wrong?"

Another nod and this time she raised her eyes to meet her mother's.

"Just keep working at it. That's what we all need to do. When Daddy or I correct you for something, try to think about it and remember for the next time. We're trying to help you grow up so that you can be the lady God wants you to be." Sarah smiled encouragingly at her daughter.

"That's what I need to do, too," Sarah told Janelle. "I'm not always a good mother, but I keep trying."

Janelle's eyes were still teary and her defenses had crumbled. "Is there anything else you wanted to talk about?" Sarah asked.

Janelle shook her head and Sarah stood up. "You may come outside when you're finished with your jobs," Sarah told her before joining the other children at the woodpile.

Finally, Janelle made her appearance outside. "What were you doing?" Sarah asked curiously.

"I swept the kitchen and signed a card," she answered mysteriously.

Gratitude and relief flowed over Sarah. For a brief moment, she wondered about the card part. But busy as moms are, she soon forgot about it.

After finishing the wood, Sarah stepped into the house. And stopped. The boots stood in a neat row on the boot tray. The kitchen floor was swept, counters wiped, and no clutter remained.

"Thank you, Janelle!" Sarah exclaimed. "It looks very neat in here. I love a clean house."

"You're welcome," Janelle answered with a smile.

At bedtime, Sarah pulled back the covers, eager to crawl between the cozy sheets. There on the pillow was an envelope. On top of the envelope, two candy canes lay taped together in the shape of a heart. On the outside of the envelope she read three words, penned in gold, swirly letters, "I Love You."

Sarah pulled out a small thank-you card. Inside, she saw tiny heart stickers scattered around the words. Silently she read: "THANK YOU for everything you have done for me. I feel very blessed that God made you my parents!! You have helped a lot through times when I felt discouraged and…grouchy. I love you VERY much. Love, Janelle."

"Thank you, God," Sarah breathed as her eyes filled with tears. She knew that rush of compassion had been from Him. *He knows how often I fail in frustration. How much I want to love my daughter. How much I want to guide her in right ways.*

A Boy and His Anger

J ANN

They were at it again! Those two boys! Diane heard thumping and loud voices. The ceiling above her shook and vibrated. Smacks and whacks reverberated down the stairs. They were to be changing their clothing, but it sounded like they were in another of those Big Fights! Diane groaned inwardly. Why couldn't they just get along? Didn't she teach them to be kind and love each other?

Loud wails drifted down the stairs. "M-O-M! He hit me with his belt!" Diane sighed and headed up the steps. She opened the bedroom door and faced them. They hadn't even started changing their clothes.

For a brief moment Diane felt utterly helpless. She felt like all her parenting ideals and "tricks of the trade" had taken wings and flown out the window. What was she to do with these ten- and thirteen-year-old boys standing there with fire dancing in their eyes? She took a deep breath and breathed a prayer.

"Boys, this is totally uncalled for. You will get changed in two minutes and get out the door for your chores. But first of all, there will be apologies." The boys' glares loosened and they said the right thing, but down underneath Diane was not convinced it was genuine.

Sanford was thirteen. It seemed lately he was restless. He often initiated these scraps with his younger brother. Sanford was fast being ushered into the world of young adulthood. He was stretching up and outgrowing his clothes. His voice was changing. He liked the feel of a shaver in his hand. He could lift things that he struggled with before. He liked running his hands over those rippling muscles in his arms. It gave him the feeling of becoming a man! It spelled power to him and that meant control. In his mind he was not a little boy anymore. So when his younger brother irked him he could handle it. He could twist David's arms behind his back in one swift motion. And he could pinch hard enough to leave a bruise. He felt bad afterward, but it gave him that feeling of control. It felt good at the time… Sanford didn't always understand the surges of anger that swept over him. One day he felt like a little boy; the next day he felt like a man.

Diane pondered these outbursts as she headed back to the kitchen. She recalled stories she had read of grown men who never learned to control their anger, and their family suffered because of this monster. It made her tremble to think of her son turning out like that. Today was her day of opportunity. She needed to think about it some more and talk with her husband. God cared too and promised wisdom if she but asked.

That evening Diane got out a pen and paper and prepared an assignment for Sanford:

Write seventy-five words minimum for each question. This must be done neatly on notebook paper and laid on Daddy's dresser by tomorrow evening.

1. What causes me to get angry, and how do I feel when I am angry?

2. What can I do to overcome getting angry?

3. Write five Bible verses on kindness and being gentle.

Diane did not see Sanford working at his assignment. But by the following evening there was a neatly folded sheet of paper lying on the dresser in her bedroom.

These were Sanford's answers:

1. I get angry because I want to get even with David for what he did to me. I don't stop and think what would happen to him if I hurt him. I don't try hard enough to be kind to him. I feel miserable and wish I would never have done what I did. I would like to put more effort forth in controlling my anger and not letting it come out on other people and harming them.

2. I can overcome my anger by praying to God and asking for help in controlling my anger. When I am tempted to get angry I must do something else to prevent myself from getting angry. I can overcome by not letting my thoughts run wild and keeping them on good ideas and not wishing to get even if I am mistreated. I am sorry for my anger and will try to do better.

continued on page 64

Teaching and Being Taught

ANOTHER OF GOD'S CHILDREN IN TRAINING

Train up a child in the way he should go: and when he is old, he will not depart from it (Proverbs 22:6).

Many times I've said, "I wish God was more specific in the Bible about child training." Then as I've been given the responsibility of training eight souls, I realize that God knows that 1+2=3 is not how we raise our children. They aren't cookie cutter copies. He is gracious and we must be too. Many times it has seemed so true what the poem titled "The School of Motherhood" says in essence that we mothers are being trained as well.

As a young mother I asked older mothers for advice and often got the answer, "We don't have any answers." My husband reminds me how disappointing that was when I wanted direction. However, after seventeen years of training children, I understand. If God doesn't give lots of specifics, maybe I shouldn't either! An older mother recently said, "We can so easily give young people wrong advice. Based on our own experience we advise people, but it may not be well rounded or fit their situation." Now, this book is a great idea, I think, especially for anyone who feels they have no one to ask or follow. But always bear in mind that God will direct a sincere seeker, and you can't apply the advice everyone gives because we only have twenty-four hours in every day! Maybe you want advice from others because you want to do things different from your parents or siblings. You don't want to make the same mistakes they did. I was recently instructed that if you set out to make sure your children don't grow up to be "thus and so" you may accomplish that well, but you may get further down the road and see what you dropped the ball on as you focused on "thus and so." One thing we can rest in as we train children is that God loves them more than we do, and we want Him and His grace to have the credit for drawing our children to Himself. We can't be perfect and neither can our children. Just remember that God gives the increase.

I found that rather than asking for open-ended advice, asking older mothers what they would do different usually brought an answer. A few responses that stand out in my memory are… "Do things with my children that they ask me to do…" "Not think that I had to sew all of their clothes…" "Spend more time with them." From that I would say you could sum it up to say that time and connection with your children is vital. So vital and yet so hard sometimes. I'm an older, more tired mother than I was with my first children and can see that young zeal is so necessary for raising children. However, growing tired helps us to see that sometimes our youthful vigor and busyness wasn't always channeled in the right direction. Maybe the pressure to make quilts like Sue, and use cloth diapers like Joy, and bake like Mary, and garden like Faith, and be frugal like Sarah, and have children who never wriggle in church and who always remember their manners, and, and, and… seems so doable because we're young and energetic. Then we end up cheating our children of the peaceful, godly mother they need. This may seem oversimplified. *But seek ye first the kingdom of God, and his righteousness; and all these things shall be added unto you* (Matthew 6:33). The ability to keep up with others won't be added, but the ability to be at peace doing God's will for our own family. I write none of this from behind a perfect family, always obedient children, and an ever-peaceful mother. Actually, I write in weakness as I see from my lack how important this is.

Stay at peace with God, your husband, and yourself, and keep your eye on the goal. You are representing God to your children. Your health (or lack thereof), energy (or lack thereof), pregnancy, housekeeping, farm help, etc. may all compete for your attention. "You need to take care of yourself because no one else will," is advice from a sister in our church, who never married, and who shares insights with me from her home life with ten siblings. "Mother always rested a little each day and did something she wanted to every day, even though we weren't so aware of it. She also had help with laundry for years." Part of being a good mother, passing on the faith, and training children is knowing your limitations and asking for help. Maybe that's a hard task. It has been for me, but it will bless you, your family, and those who get to help you. Even being humbled by having someone see our messy house isn't all bad.

Try to remember to work joyfully with your husband and not compare yourselves among yourselves. It isn't wise. Ask God for wisdom for *your* situation and He'll speak. Maybe neighbors down the road have an orderly life. They always have an evening routine and devotions at 7:45, then bedtime at 8:30, and that looks lovely to you, to help the children calm down and know what to expect. However, your hubby says, "Evening is my time with the children; they don't have to go to bed early." You aren't married to the neighbor, and maybe it's selfishness that wants everyone to go to bed, so it's quiet. Oops, you forgot part of the equation too—neighbor's hubby gets up at four o'clock and gets home at three or four in the afternoon. So what does all that have to do with child training? As we seek God for help with Johnny's problem, we may not feel like we're getting answers, but God may be working on me first.

Now, I really like lists—practical ones—and have wished that simple daily list could take the guesswork out of motherhood. I haven't heard of anyone finding a list like that yet. Here's just a random list of advice I've found valuable. Is it always easy? Have I always followed the right advice? No! Shall we keep on, a day at a time? Yes!

• Be consistent.

• Do jobs with your children when you can (especially large ones).

• Say what you mean and mean what you say.

• Have some lines you fall back to when needed. Repeat often. Children may act annoyed, but they'll remember.

"A job worth doing is worth doing right."

"If at first you don't succeed, try, try again."

"Kindness is a golden key."

"Don't count your chickens before they hatch."

"Do unto others as you would have them do unto you."

"Always be nice."

"God loves you, and so do I!"

• Choose your battles. Keep your expectations simple to remember.

• Children won't do things you don't allow. (This is obviously young children.)

• Find advice in Proverbs. They tell us what God thinks on practicals.

• "When a child knows what to do with a hairbrush, he's old enough to be spanked." (Advice from my grandma who was born in the early 1900s.)

• "You know, sometimes children need love in place of fussing." (Advice from my husband's grandma when she had dementia and was spending the day with us. I was fussing at my son—she was patient and he was listening to her!)

• Practice with a two-year-old following the simple command, "Come." Call them randomly from play and expect obedience. Give affirmation and let them resume playing.

In child training we need to be teachable so we can be teachers.

The husbandman that laboureth must be first partaker of the fruits. Consider what I say; and the Lord give thee understanding in all things (II Timothy 2:6-7).

Train up a child in the way he should go... A minister once put emphasis on "in the way." We parents must be in the Way. What a responsibility, calling, journey, school, blessing, and the list could go on. Take heart and lean on God's everlasting arms.

A Boy and His Anger continued from page 62

3. *And be ye kind one to another, tenderhearted, forgiving one another, even as God for Christ's sake hath forgiven you* (Ephesians 4:32).

Thou shalt not avenge, nor bear any grudge against the children of thy people, but thou shalt love thy neighbour as thyself (Leviticus 19:18).

This is my commandment, That ye love one another, as I have loved you (John 15:12).

And the servant of the Lord must not strive; but be gentle unto all men, apt to teach, patient (II Timothy 2:24).

To speak evil of no man, to be no brawlers, but gentle, shewing all meekness unto all men (Titus 3:2).

It touched Diane's heart to read Sanford's answers. Inside this macho boy was a tender spirit that needed guidance and nurturing. It seemed like an overwhelming task. It was not all mastered in a few weeks or months, but Diane could see signs of improvement in her soon-to-be-teenage son. She realized that by God's grace he had turned into a kindhearted gentle young man.